Do It Yourself
Home Maintenance
and Repairs

By the same author

Painting and Decorating
Building a Beautiful Garden
Making the Most of a Small Home
Making the Most of Colour in the Home
Making the Most of Your Pension
Do It Yourself Home Improvements (in preparation)

as joint author
Newnes Practical Householder Encyclopedia

as editor
Life Cycle of a Product
Marketing in the 70s

Alan Taylor

Do It Yourself Home Maintenance and Repairs

MacGibbon & Kee   London

Granada Publishing Limited
First published in Great Britain 1972 by MacGibbon & Kee Ltd
3 Upper James Street London W1R 4BP

ISBN 0 261 10013 0

Filmset in Photon Times 12 pt. by
Richard Clay (The Chaucer Press) Ltd, Bungay, Suffolk
and printed in Great Britain by
Fletcher & Son Ltd, Norwich

Contents

	page
List of Illustrations	ix
Foreword	xi

1 **Roofs, Chimneys, Gutters and Downpipes**   1
Roofs Chimneys Gutters and downpipes More on
ladders

2 **Outside Walls**   8
Repointing Spalling Rendered walls Stucco Outhouses
Structural stains Important note

3 **Interior Walls**   17
Stains Replastering

4 **Floors and Ceilings**   25
Underlay for carpeting Squeaky floorboards Carpets
Stains on carpets Floor tiles Vinyl flooring Ceilings
Polystyrene

5 **Fireplaces**   35
Smoky chimney Cracked fireback Cracked hearth
Stained and cracked chimney breast

6 **Doors**   41
Unsticking Sheathing Painting doors

7 **Windows**   47
Sashcords Replacing broken panes Corroded metal
windows Peeling paint Frames Sills Leaded windows

page

8 **Bathrooms and kitchens**   59
   Damage from steam Bath care Tile care Basins and
   water closets Kitchen and bathroom furniture Fitting a
   canopy Fitting an extractor fan

9 **Halls and Stairways**   68
   Ladders and scaffolding Squeaking stairs Carpeting
   stairs Colours

10 **Damp Walls and Ceilings**   73
   Causes of damp Condensation Pattern staining Paint-
   ing and condensation Rain penetration The roof
   Faulty damp-proof course Interstitial damage

11 **Rot in Timber**   85

12 **Woodworm**   89
   Damage done Types of beetle Diagnosis and treatment Structural timbers Floors Precautions

13 **Simple Electrical Work**   100
   Do's and don'ts Definitions Reading a meter Fuses
   Distribution Adaptors Tracing faults

14 **Simple Plumbing**   108
   The basic plumbing system Frost precautions Tap
   washers Ballvalves Water hammer Blocked sinks
   Drains

15 **Spring Cleaning**   118
   The annual clean Cleaning metal surfaces Windows
   Outside work Checklist

16 **Furniture Renovation**   125
   Some basic principles Chairs Previously painted
   furniture Wicker furniture Painting previous stained
   furniture Bleaching Cigarette burns Complete re-
   finishing Limed oak Dents and chips Freshening up
   polished furniture Dyeing wood Picture frames Brass
   and copper

17 **First Aid for Fences**   135

Appendix:
1 Decorating Materials   140
   Materials for various surfaces Primers Painting over
   previously painted surfaces

page

2   Specifications for the Treatment of Rot in Wood   146
      Full dry rot treatment   Full wet rot treatment

3   Metrication   149

Product Index   151

Index   161

List of Illustrations

Fig.		*page*
1	Cat ladder on roof attached to pole ladder	2
2	Hawk	9
3	Jointing and pointing	9
4	Bucket and roller	11
5	Plasterer's trowels	23
6	Turning and rolling fitted carpet	27
7	Tiling a floor	30
8	Dry ceiling join	33
9	Parts of a chimney	38
10	Sticking doors	42
11	Threshold draught strip	43
12	Procedure for painting sheathed and panelled doors	45
13	Causes of a sash window sticking	47
14	Mending sash cords	49
15	Causes of sashes not closing properly	50
16	Glazing	52
17	Moisture damage to sashes and sills	56
18	Improvised scaffolding	61
19	Cutting glass for an extractor fan	67
20	Construction of stairs	69
21	Carpeting of stairs	71
22	Lutings, drip channels and rectifying a badly sloped sill	79
23	Damp in several places caused by misplaced or broken roofing tile	81
24	Interstitial condensation	84
25	Eradicating woodworm in attic	96

Fig.
		page
26	Electric meter, fuse and plugs	102
27	Pipe layout	109
28	Protection for outlet pipe to hopper	110
29	Tap construction	112
30	Cistern construction	114
31	Drainage layout	117
32	Repairing and reseating kitchen chair	126
33	First aid for fence	137

Foreword

A house is like a human body inasmuch as something goes wrong
with it now and then. It gets a headache (a loose tile on the roof). Its
feet hurt (faulty damp proof course). It suffers from indigestion
(damp patches on walls). It becomes tired and listless (decorations
want cleaning and renewing). And as with the human body, if you
attend to these ailments in time you can often obviate the necessity
for expensive and tiresome surgery.

This book does not pretend to be an exhaustive treatise on the
subject, with the many skills entailed. My aim has been to cover all
the simple jobs involved in keeping a home in good condition, pointing out when a job is likely to be dangerous or of sufficient magni-
tude to enlist the services of a professional. This book is rather
like the one on home doctoring that every wise mother keeps at hand,
or like a cookery book that is glanced at when nobody else is around
to point a finger at one's lack of knowledge.

Asterisked words will be found in the Product Index with the
names of proprietary products and addresses of manufacturers, who
will of course be willing in most cases to answer queries or to supply
instructional literature.

I should like to thank P. L. G. Bateman of Rentokil Laboratories
Ltd for technically vetting Chapters 11 and 12; Leslie G. Smith,
CEng, MIEE for checking Chapter 13; Dr Norman E. Hickin, PhD,
BSc, FRES for supplying matter for Appendix 2; Denis Gray, who
has allowed me to include the table on page 144, which originally
appeared in an article contributed by me to the magazine *Practical
Householder*.

A. T.

1
Roofs, Chimneys, Gutters and Downpipes

Roofs

A roof is generally the most neglected part of a house. A chimney is too, until attention is drawn to it by smoke belching forth into a living room. Roofs and chimneys need scaffolding or a cat ladder to reach them, and as most people dislike heights, only small items of their maintenance are within the scope of any but the most dedicated of do-it-yourselfers.

A cat ladder, or crawling board, provides firm footing and distributes a person's weight over a roof. It is lashed to an extension or pole ladder standing on the ground, which in turn is lashed to convenient projections in the eaves, such as gutter brackets or an eyescrew driven into the fascia board. Alternatively, a colleague may stand on the extension or pole ladder at near eaves height, so as to prevent it from being pushed backwards. The top of the cat ladder may be secured by hooks gripping the ridge of the roof (Fig. 1).

A damp patch (see Chapter 10) inside a house may indicate that there is something wrong with the roof — maybe broken tiles — or faulty chimney stack, flaunching or flashing. To save the trouble of climbing onto the roof for inspection, you can often detect faults through binoculars from the garden.

A broken single-lap tile in a roof which is not boarded or felted underneath may be replaced by climbing into the loft, lifting the damaged tile so that the nibs disengage from the

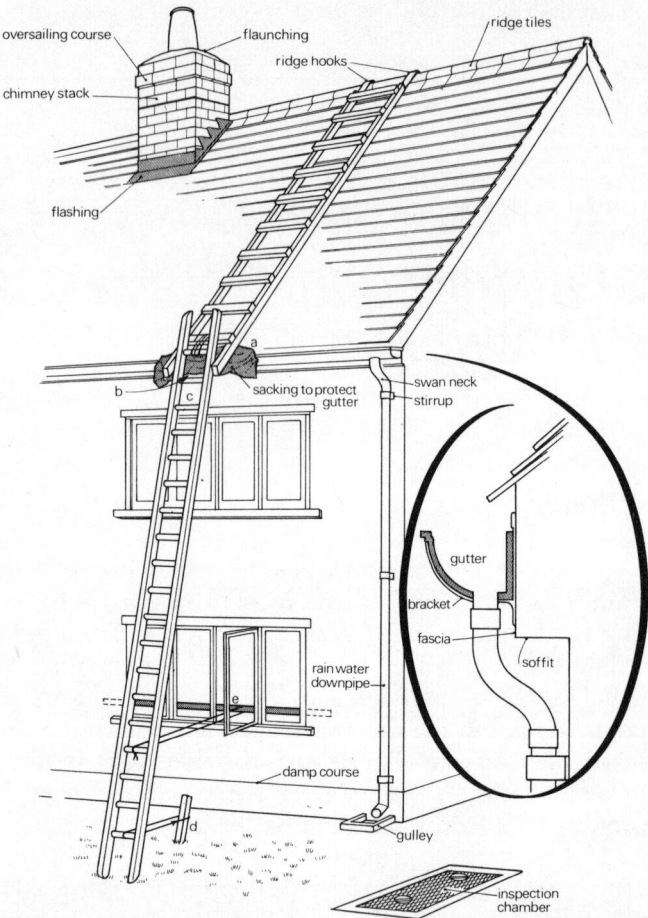

Fig. 1. Outside of a house, with cat ladder or crawling board attached to a builder's ladder. (a) If no ridge hooks, tie foot of cat ladder or crawling board to top of ladder. (b) Secure top of ladder to eye screws driven into fascia, or (c) a colleague should stand near the top of the ladder to balance your weight on the crawling board. (d) Tie foot of ladder to stake driven into ground, or (e) to a batten inside window frame

tiling batten, removing it and hooking on a new one. This has to be done carefully or adjoining tiles will be displaced. Most roofs are double- or triple-lapped and boarded or felted to keep out wind and snow. Repairs in these cases must be undertaken from the outside.

A slate that is merely cracked can be made waterproof by lifting the lower edge with a builder's trowel and inserting a piece of zinc sheeting. When the trowel is removed the weight of the slate will keep the zinc in position.

To remove nailed slates, insert a ripper (which consists of a narrow length of steel with a T-shaped cutting edge at the end) under the tile, feel for the nail and give a sharp pull. If this will not do the job, break the slate and hook on a new one with a tingle (a clip nailed to the appropriate roofing batten). Or use a narrow strip of zinc bent at the top to engage with the batten. Place the new slate in position and bend the lower end of the zinc over it.

Roofs are not often painted in Britain. If you are really colour-conscious you can add the hue you want and at the same time lengthen the life of the roof by coating it with a roof paint*.

Chimneys

Acid fumes from fires will eventually penetrate the bricks of a chimney and disrupt the pointing. Frost will add to the damage and the chimney will tend to lean (see page 37). If your chimney stacks are not vertical call in a contractor to put matters right, or a high wind may blow the whole lot down. Flue stains on the outside rendering of a chimney stack are unsightly; seal them in with aluminium primer sealer before painting with cement, emulsion or stone paint.

It is almost impossible to get rid of bad smoke stains on a brick chimney that is *not* rendered because the inside of the bricks will be black, and sealer and paint will be out of place. If the stains are only slight, however, you might try cleaning with water and a stiff brush. Don't use detergent or any other chemical, or efflorescence may occur. Then apply a brick dye*.

Gutters and Downpipes

Clear rainwater gutters with a garden trowel once a year – in late autumn after leaves have ceased to fall and before really severe weather sets in. The debris will be rich in bird lime, so tip it round your rose trees rather than into the ashpan.

Gutters and downpipes may be of galvanised iron, asbestos or plastic.

Those of galvanised iron will last for several years without protection, but the coating of zinc, which is applied by a hot-dip process, will eventually wear, causing the exposed metal to rust. Quite apart from this, unpainted galvanised iron looks extremely ugly. To paint *new* galvanised iron, rub it down with white spirit[1] and apply a coat of calcium plumbate primer. For the inside of a gutter, which is not seen, use two coats of black bituminous paint over the primer; this is cheap and waterproof. For the outside apply an undercoat and two finishing coats of an alkyd resin paint* of the same colour as the walls – and the gutter will not be noticed.

It is, of course, possible to form a visual border between roof and walls by using a different colour on the guttering. With modern houses of severe design, breaking up a plain flat frontage often avoids monotony and adds attraction. For instance, a white wall and a green roof would take battleship grey guttering. Green might be considered suitable against brick-red walls and a red roof.

If you are thinking of carrying out such a scheme, bear in mind that the eye tends to follow a straight line beyond its extremities, so that a gutter picked out in a separate colour will make the house appear more squat (wider and not so high). An opposite effect will be achieved by painting downpipes in a different colour. Here the eye will be directed over the top of the pipes, making the roof look higher and the walls narrower.

To paint behind new galvanised iron downpipes that are

[1] To the British, white spirit is a cheap and efficient substitute for turpentine. British decorators prefer the term *white spirit* to *turpentine substitute* because the latter is regarded as not being sufficiently definitive. In some countries, notably Australia and New Zealand, white spirit denotes something different – such as unrefined benzine – and this should not, for safety sake, be used. Where references to *white spirit* occur in this book, will readers in these countries kindly translate to their more familiar expression *turpentine substitute*.

The liquid that should be used, whether called *white spirit* or *turpentine substitute* is inflammable but not dangerously so. It is the liquid normally used for thinning oil paint and cleaning paint brushes.

already fixed, soak a piece of cloth in paint, pass it round the back and pull to and fro. Protect the wall with a sheet of cardboard inserted behind.

Scrape or wirebrush off as much rust as you can from an *old* gutter, touch in bared parts with an anti-rust compound* and give the whole lot a coat of zinc chromate primer before using bituminous paint inside, and undercoat and finishing coats of alkyd resin paint outside. Some compounds act as a primer as well as a rust neutraliser. With these, all you need to do is to follow on with undercoat and finishing coats. With others again, no undercoat is needed. To remove rust from behind a pipe, pass a piece of abrasive paper round the back and pull it to and fro in the same way as has been explained for painting.

Cleaning inside a downpipe is a fiddling job not to be undertaken unless you are a perfectionist and prepared to devote a considerable amount of time to it. Here is one way of tackling the job.

Climb aloft and drop a long length of string, with a weight attached to it, down the pipe. Attach a rope to the other end of the string and pull it through. Tie a pot scourer to the middle of the rope and draw it up and down to get rid of dirt deposits.

Now remove the scourer and tie a bunched-up cloth in its place. Pull the rope down steadily and at the same time get a colleague to pour bituminous paint in at the top. Then pull the rope up and down quickly two or three times to distribute the paint evenly.

The cloth will have to be carefully cut to the correct dimensions so that it will 'hug' the sides of the pipe without sticking.

If there is a hole in a pipe or gutter, clean it out with a cylindrical file and patch with one of the proprietary plastic metal stoppers*.

To mend a leaking joint in a gutter, unscrew the retaining bolt and lift. Scrape out the old jointing compound and replace with new before bolting up again. You may have to saw off a badly rusted bolt and use a new one when refixing. Check the flow of the gutter by pouring in water at the highest point from a garden watering can.

When a bracket holding a gutter breaks you can fix a gutter repair bracket, obtainable at a hardware shop or builder's merchant, and fit it alongside the old one, thus obviating the necessity for renewal.

Asbestos is absorbent and contains an extremely high proportion of alkali salts. If an asbestos gutter is left unpainted, the moisture it has absorbed will expand on freezing, causing the surface to become powdery. If it is painted with an oil paint, water will bring the salts to the surface where they will mingle with the oil and form a crude soap which will soften the paint-film and cause it to lift and peel. To an extent this can be prevented by applying a coat of alkali-resisting primer; but it is far safer not to use any paint containing oil.

Bituminous paint is fairly alkali-resisting; so is an outdoor grade of emulsion paint*. Apply these direct to asbestos gutters and pipes, after they have been brushed down, without using any primer. Thin the first coat of emulsion with the same quantity of water to fill the pores and then follow with a second normal coat.

Plastic pipes are self-coloured and are not intended to be painted. For this reason their advantage of lightness, which simplifies fixing and repairs, is counterbalanced by the disadvantage of not being able to change the colour scheme of the outside of the house if you wish to do so – though gutters made of polyvinyl chloride (PVC) may be given a couple of thin finishing coats.

More on Ladders

When an extension ladder, up to 16 ft closed, is fully extended it should have at least two rungs overlapping; for a closed length of between 17 and 20 ft – three rungs; anything over 21 ft (which you are not likely to use) – four rungs. Set the ladder on firm ground at an angle of about 70 degrees from ground level. If you do not have a colleague to stand on the bottom rung to prevent slipping while you are working aloft, secure the foot by one of the methods shown in Fig. 1. (At the time of writing, ladder lengths have not yet been metricated.)

After securing loose or flapping clothing and tucking trouser bottoms inside socks, mount cautiously, looking straight at the wall in front of you – not up or down or you may become giddy. Don't be alarmed at the ladder's whipping under your weight. If it did not 'give' it would snap.

On reaching the top of the ladder, tie one of the top rungs to a gutter bracket or eyescrew driven into the fascia board. Don't rest the ladder on a rainwater gutter unless, as in the case in Fig. 1, there is no other way out. In that case, protect the gutter with sacking.

Aluminium ladders are less than half the weight of wooden ones and so easier to handle; but they are twice the price. A disadvantage is that they tend to slip at the top unless secured extra well. Some makes have rubber or composition pads attached to the foot of the strings (upright pieces) to prevent slipping at ground level.

Don't paint a wooden ladder – varnish it or protect it with timber preservative. Store it in the dry where air can circulate. Don't leave it to bend under its own weight: if you are hanging it horizontally on staples driven into a wall, have one or two more staples in between to support the middle.

Keep a ladder under lock and key. It would be a gift on a plate for a burglar!

2
Outside
Walls

Repointing

Two main defects likely to develop in the brick wall of a house are decayed pointing and disintegration of the bricks through frost and efflorescence – known as spalling.

Repointing a wall is a big job, consisting of raking out the joints between the bricks for at least $\frac{1}{2}$ in. (12 mm.) or until firm mortar is reached, and replacing it with fresh mortar mixed stiff and to approximately the same density as the brick. This mortar should be about one part of cement by volume to between five and six parts of sand, with one of hydrated powder lime to make the mix workable. An alternative to lime is a proprietary plasticiser obtainable at do-it-yourself shops and builders' merchants.

A thin surface pointing is of no use whatever; it will soon crack and fall out. Doing the job in depth without staining the bricks requires practice; so, to start with at any rate, keep a clean wet cloth handy to wipe off droppings. Use a cold chisel and hammer for raking, or an old worn screwdriver with a metal handle to take hammer blows. You can, of course, get an attachment to fit an electric drill, and this will do the work much more quickly.

Before pointing, brush out the raked cavity between the bricks and wet it by swishing water in with a brush. Don't oversoak.

You can get specially shaped tools for pointing; a small plasterer's trowel is as good as any. Make a hawk, to hold the mortar, using a flat piece of wood or hardboard about 300 mm. or a foot square. Screw this through the centre into a piece of dowelling about 25 mm. (1 in.) in diameter and 200 mm. (8 or 9 in.) long and this will serve as a handle; a piece of broomstick is ideal for the purpose (Fig. 2).

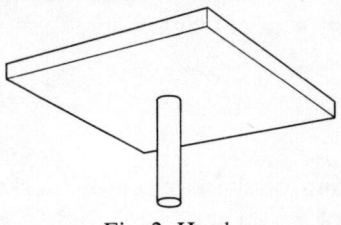

Fig. 2. Hawk

Put a dab of mortar on the hawk and flatten it with the trowel until it is about the same thickness as the gap between the bricks. Hold the hawk close to the wall and cut off a strip of the mix of width approximately equal to the depth of the gap. Take the strip on the edge of the trowel and press it firmly in, holding the hawk underneath and against the wall to catch any droppings. Finishing can be done in any one of the ways shown in Fig. 3, dipping the trowel in water first. The hollow joint

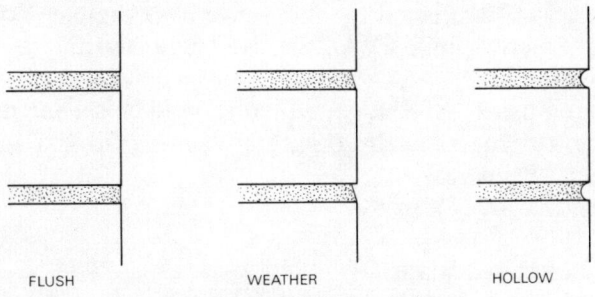

FLUSH   WEATHER   HOLLOW

Fig. 3. Jointing and pointing

may be achieved by wiping it with a piece cut from an old galvanised bucket handle. Make sure that the top of the brick under each joint does not form a ledge or it will collect rain which will eventually saturate it.

Fill a metre (yard) or so of vertical joints first and then attend to the horizontal ones.

When a metre of brickwork has been completed, place a straight edge up to the jointing (a batten of wood will do) and draw a blunt knife across to cut off any overhang of mortar.

As has already been said, complete repointing is a big job; but if the mortar has deteriorated in only a few places these parts can quickly be patched up, using a colour additive in new mortar to match in with existing work.

Spalling

Spalling is a flaking of the surface of brickwork. It can take place at any part of a wall and is generally seen close to ground level where rain splashes up, particularly at the part of the wall immediately under the damp-proof course.

There is no need to cut out a spalled brick completely. Rake away two or three inches of the surface with a cold chisel and hammer, cut a new brick to the required thickness and stick it into the cavity with mortar.

Epoxy resin adhesive * may be used instead of mortar; but if the cut brick is not of the exact size, or the adjoining surfaces are uneven, you will not be able to fill the gap as you can with mortar. Epoxy resin is considerably more expensive, but if only a few bricks are affected the difference is negligible. You may, as an alternative, mix PVA adhesive * with mortar to make a super-firm joint.

To cut a brick, score it round with a cold chisel and hammer and give it a smart tap. If you are not successful you will have to obtain a brick saw.

Rendered Walls

A cement or masonry paint * will fill hair cracks in a rendered wall. Wider cracks should be undercut. Brush out the cavity with a soft brush and fill with mortar mixed no stronger than that of the rendering. You will not be far wrong if you take one part cement, five of sand and one of hydrated powder lime by volume. Proprietary plasticiser can take the place of the lime. Make two applications of the filler rather than attempting to do the job in one operation.

When repairing a roughcast wall (one covered with a mix containing small stones) or a Tyrolean-finished wall (where the mix has been applied by a special gun) the bumpy effect can be achieved by placing a wooden float over the filling and pulling it away quickly; then by titivating it by hand so that the relief pattern is uniform with that of the remainder of the wall. Repair pebbledash (a rendering where the small stones are thrown onto the wet mortar surface so that they are exposed and are not an integral part of the mix) by sticking the stones into the wet filling by hand. Level off by placing a flat board across the filling, each end being pressed closely against the surrounding firm pebbledash.

In addition to cement and masonry paint, rendered walls may be finished in an outdoor grade of emulsion paint*. The first two will protect a porous wall against rain. Emulsion provides decoration only, though some have waterproofers added.

Cement paint will ruin a good distemper brush by solidifying in the stock; so use a cheap brush which can be thrown away after the job is finished. Emulsion is quickly applied with a lambswool roller – which has a long pile to reach interstices. Obviously you cannot very well carry the usual

Fig. 4. Bucket and roller

type of paint tray up a ladder, so pour the paint into a bucket and stand a short piece of wood in it to roller out before use (Fig. 4). An old biscuit tin with a hole punched in two opposing sides for insertion of a wire handle will do equally as well.

A snag about these make-do contraptions is that, when hooked onto a rung of a ladder, they are often out of reach. And when the roller is dipped in, they tend to swing, making rollering-out difficult. A specially designed scuttle* is now on the market which locks onto the ladder strings at the right height and without movement. It is also useful for holding tools when working at a height.

The wall paints mentioned require their own primer or sealer recommended by the manufacturer.

Stucco

The old type of wall finish known as stucco is softer than modern renderings and requires a weaker mix – more than the usual five parts of sand to one of cement – for patching. It should not be sealed by a paint coating that is too impervious. Old-fashioned paints on a vegetable oil base, which do not set too hard, are best because they require less preparatory cleaning and scraping of the surfaces. (See Product Index: *Masonry paints for doubtful surfaces*.)

Timber Cladding

Timber wall cladding and garden furniture may be painted with primer, undercoat and two finishing coats of an alkyd resin paint* or, if it is wished to retain the natural grain, by giving it three coats of an ultra violet ray absorbing varnish*. Ordinary wood varnishes, even the superior yacht varnish, are of little use because they contain no pigment to obstruct the damaging rays of the sun and so will last for only about one season.

Most U.V. absorbing varnishes, on the other hand, contain pigment whose refractive index is the same as that of the medium – thus keeping it transparent.

Outhouses

Under the heading *Gutters and Downpipes* in Chapter 1 you will see how asbestos is painted, and the same rules apply to an asbestos shed or garage. Being waterproof, bituminous paint is suitable for the roof — venetian red, to make it look like tiles, or green to mingle with the surrounding foliage. An outdoor grade of emulsion paint* might be best for the walls because you can get it in a variety of colours to match the house decoration.

Make sure that all mossy growths are wirebrushed off and, if they are obstinate, treat green patches with a fungicide, obtainable at a good paint shop. Ordinary household bleach will also serve the purpose — washed off with clear water before painting. For extensive algae growths, mix zinc or magnesium silico-fluoride* in water (about 25 grammes to a litre). To estimate the amount of chemical to order, see how far a litre of plain water will go over the surface and multiply the number of times this measurement will go into the entire surface by 25. If you are working in imperial measure, the quantity is 4 oz. of fluoride to a gallon of water, and your estimated spreading power will therefore be: area covered by 1 gallon of plain water multiplied by 4.

When an impervious finish is applied to the outside only of asbestos sheeting and not to the back, the sheeting may warp or crack owing to differential carbonation; so paint the inside surface as well. If the roofing bolts let in water, unscrew and insert a mastic compound* between the head and the washer.

New concrete building slabs are often greasy, owing to the release agent used in moulding them. If you decide to colour the surface, allow six or twelve months to elapse before decorating with emulsion, stone or cement paint — to allow the agent to leach out and disperse. If any remains, scrub with white spirit. (See footnote on page 4.)

Structural Stains

Here are a few of the commonest stains seen on an outside wall, and the most effective way of treating them:

Copper stains. Water from copper fittings leaking onto a painted surface can cause nasty green stains. Treat with a weak solution of hydrogen peroxide followed by a clear water rinse.

Iron stains, often seen on metal studded doors. Remove with citric acid or lemon juice.

Rust stains on concrete. Try the following remedies in this order: (1) Citric acid or lemon. (2) Bleaching solution mixed with whiting to form a poultice. (3) Wet the surface and apply a 10 per cent solution of phosphoric or hydrochloric acid. *See the important note on the mixing and handling of acids at the end of this chapter.*

Nail-head staining. When ferrous nails are driven into oak, a grey pattern may appear on the surface, owing to reaction between the iron and the acid in the timber. Bleach the stains with hydrogen peroxide and sink the heads well below the surface, filling the apertures with hard stopping*. Prevent this happening in new work by using non-ferrous fittings.

Bronze stains on masonry. Provided the stains have not sunk in too deeply, they may be removed by applying a poultice comprising one part by volume of ammonium chloride and four parts of powdered talc. Brush off when dry and repeat several times.

Concrete stains on brick. Wirebrush and treat with mixic acid*.

Cement splashes on bricks. Try vinegar. If this is not effective, use a 10 per cent solution of hydrochloric or mixic acid and wash down afterwards. *See important note at the end of this chapter.*

Paint splashes on bricks and stone. Paint stripper* will remove the surface paint. To get the remainder out of the pores, give another application and use a wire brush, or rub with a cut stone or brick of the same texture; or rub with a carborundum block or emery cloth. As a final resort, apply a poultice of ammonia and whiting. If, after all these efforts, specks of coloured paint still remain, coat the surface with well-thinned emulsion paint of the same colour as the brick or stone and wipe off while still wet. What is left will cover the specks in the interstices.

Tar stains. When an oil paint is applied over tar splashes or a previously bituminous or creosoted surface, the solvents in the paint will activate the underlying material and cause it to bleed through. Emulsion paint is not likely to affect the underlying material in this way but, being hard, it may craze over such a relatively soft surface. If oil paint is used, the old surface should be sealed in first with aluminium primer sealer or a proprietary sealer*.

Cleaning bathstone. As the large-scale application of steam for the removal of atmosphere deposits is out of the question for the walls of a small house, soak the surface continuously with water and brush with a stiff brush to remove the calcium sulphate and carbonate which form on exposure.

Patchy discoloration on stripped stonework. When an oil paint-film is stripped from porous stone, some oil from the paint may be left behind on the softer and more spongy parts; dirt is attracted and a dark stain is left. Apply a poultice of sifted whiting and acetone, and keep the mix moist for half an hour or so by adding more acetone.

Sulphate attack on brickwork. Sometimes horizontal fissures, wider than hair cracks, appear in a rendered wall. These can be the result of expansion caused by chemicals in the rendering and the fault can be diagnosed by examining the back of detached pieces of rendering to see if sulphate crystals are adhering. The remedy lies in the hands of a good builder or surveyor.

Chalking. The ultra-violet rays of the sun will eventually cause the medium in an oil paint, particularly a white one, to thin out, leaving fine pigment particles on the surface. These dull a high gloss but, when they are washed off, a clean bright surface is left behind. So long as chalking is not too pronounced it is an advantage not an evil, because dirt mingles with the pigment powder and is easily removed. This causes the paintfilm to become thinner and subsequent coats of paint will not build up to make too heavy a layer.

Important Note

In all cases where acid is used in a diluted form add the acid to water, not water to the acid. Protect the eyes with goggles and hands with rubber gloves, and if the skin does get splashed apply plenty of cold water quickly. Do not allow any waste to go down the drain. You can spread lime on the ground to neutralise the droppings.

3
Interior
Walls

Stains

Of the many decorative materials that can be used on living-room walls those that come most readily to mind are paper, vinyl* and poly-ethylene* coverings and emulsion. Wallpaper lends a warm, homely atmosphere to a room and gives a wide choice of patterns. On the other hand, emulsion paint is easier to keep clean. It can be washed and even scrubbed; and if a child starts to exercise his or her artistic talents with a biro pen, a wallpaper will be ruined, whereas the ink can be erased from emulsion paint with methylated spirit mixed with an equal quantity of water (to slow down evaporation). Vinyls and poly-ethylenes also provide pattern and are easily cleaned.

There is not much difference in the time required for working with any of these wall-covering materials, though in rooms with a lot of corners and obstructions paint would have the edge over paper.

As paper can cost from a few pence to as many pounds, it is difficult to assess which would be the cheaper. Taking an average good paper at 75p–£1 a roll, and allowing for two coats of emulsion, the cost would work out approximately the same. Vinyl and poly-ethylene are generally more expensive.

The stains we have dealt with on outside walls are serious only to the fussy. Indeed, some may want to produce a stain deliberately on, say, a garden wall to make it look more mellow; algae and other organic growths may be encouraged by washing down with skimmed milk, cow dung and water, or even urine. Inside, of course, it is different.

What was said in Chapter 2 on many outside stains also applies inside. Further information will now be given. Stains can be divided into three categories: (1) those that wash off, (2) those that cannot be washed off, (3) those that can be washed off but will return if their cause is not eradicated.

The first class is dealt with in Chapter 15, *Spring Cleaning*. Stains of the second class require sealing over; and this can be done by hanging a metal-backed lining paper – in which case the whole wall will have to be covered unless you can 'feather' away the step at the edges with abrasive paper. If the stain is confined only to a small area, touch over it with aluminium primer sealer, allowing a generous margin all round. Both these materials will take paint and wallpaper on top.

In the third category comes damp. If you paint over a wet surface, the water will soon penetrate the new decoration and the stain will return – if it does not push the paint or paper off in the meantime. Damp walls are dealt with in Chapter 10.

Once the cause of damp has been discovered and put right you will still be left with the original stain which will show either as a light patch caused by bleaching, or as a dark one – the result of dust mingling with the water. You may be able to clean this off well enough to paint or paper directly over. If not, seal it in with aluminium primer sealer.

It will be seen that the divisions into which stains fall are not tightly pigeon-holed. They may be confined to one category or may involve all three.

Always find out the cause of a stain first; then you can deal with the problem intelligently and efficiently. Quite recently we were involved in a case which at first defied diagnosis. A horizontal dark line appeared at waist height on a kitchen wall which consisted of a thin partition. In the next room was a dado surmounted by wooden moulding. In washing the wall of that room the housewife had allowed dirty water to run behind the moulding. This had been drawn through to the kitchen side by condensation which had wetted the wall sufficiently to act in the same way as a damped sheet of blotting paper acts on spilt ink.

Here are some causes of internal wall stains which may at first appear obscure but which in practice keep cropping up with monotonous regularity.

Mould. There are countless millions of mould spores floating in the atmosphere awaiting an opportunity to settle upon a surface that provides food, warmth and moisture and that is not lit too strongly. They can lie dormant for years, germinating when atmospheric conditions are favourable. The walls and ceiling of a kitchen and bathroom (see Chapter 8), and also of a living room where there is condensation, make ideal nurseries for the pest.

Mould may be identified by examining it under a powerful magnifying glass – to see if it has hyphae in the form of microscopic hairy tentacles running along the plaster surrounding each patch. These tentacles should not be confused with the furriness of efflorescence (see page 20). They eventually join up with one another, turning several small spots into one large one. The trouble is not serious as is the case with the dry-rot fungus (Chapter 11), but it will leave a dirty mark if not attended to and will ruin decorations.

Wash off the stain with an abrasive cleaner, and apply a mould inhibitor * all over the surface, not just where the stain is. Leave for a week to see whether any fresh outbreak develops. If so, repeat the dose. Then you can redecorate with any material you please – paint or wallpaper.

A process taking longer is to dilute ordinary household hypochlorate bleach with water and rub on for between ten and fifteen minutes. Then rinse and allow twenty-four hours for drying. This not only kills the spores but also bleaches discoloration. Copper sulphate solution is often used as an alternative, but it has the disadvantage that it can produce other stains.

Another way of treating the fault is to apply a paint containing a fungicide. Unfortunately, with most materials of this kind the chemical leaches out in time.

Black specks on an oil-painted wall. This trouble is often caused when oil paint is brushed onto a wall that has previously been lined with pitch paper – perhaps in an attempt to seal off damp. The cause of the damp has subsequently been cured and the pitch paper stripped off. During removal it may have left specks of tar in the interstices and these will become activated by the solvents in the new paint. If the wall had been papered instead of being oil-painted, or if a water-based paint had been used, this trouble would not be so likely to happen.

A similar fault often occurs with old paper printed in metallic inks or in a deep red.

The remedy is to seal over the surface as has already been described.

Efflorescence. This starts with paint breaking out in a rash of pimples which burst and show jagged edges. It is caused by moisture dissolving alkali salts, consisting generally of sodium, magnesium or potassium chloride present in the plaster or in the mortar joins of damp bricks. The salts leach out in a way similar to those in asbestos (page 6). On unpainted plaster, the fault shows as a white furriness.

When you move into a newly built house the plaster walls will *appear* dry after a few weeks because water will come to the surface gradually and immediately evaporate. By sealing it in with oil paint you will hinder this action and store up trouble under the paintfilm; wallpaper will become stained and the paste underneath will be adulterated. It takes approximately one month for every 25 mm. (1 in.) of wall thickness to dry out properly. That is to say, a 9 in. (225 mm. approx.) solid brick wall will remain dangerously wet for nine months – more or less according to weather conditions. A cavity wall will take less, but not much less because the air in the cavity will be dampened by the outer layer of bricks and this dampness will affect the inner layer.

The ideal would be to leave a new wall undecorated during this period, wiping off the salts as they appear with a dry cloth. Don't use water or you will drive them back in.

If you *must* have decoration on a new wall, apply a thin coat of emulsion paint which, being fairly porous, will allow the moisture to permeate through to the surface where the deposited salts may be wiped off. Emulsion is also alkali-resisting. Even emulsion can be affected, however, but after the drying-out period it can be brushed down with a stiff brush to remove any peeling parts before applying a more permanent form of decoration.

Efflorescence will not cause trouble unless the structure is damp. You can test whether a wall is dry by attaching a small sheet of glass with Sellotape and leaving it in that position for twenty-four hours to see if beads of moisture collect on the undersurface. If you are not absolutely sure that all traces have disappeared, apply a coat of alkali-resisting primer or brush on a 14 per cent solution, by weight, of calcium chloride in water.

These materials are not an absolutely sure cure for the trouble. They only help.

Spalling of plaster. When examining the pimples caused by efflorescence, make sure it is only the paint that is affected and not the underlying plaster. If the latter, it may be that unslaked lime is expanding or that too much water was used in an early stage of trowelling. The only remedy here is to scrape off the excrescences, brush well down and reskim the craters.

If new plaster becomes friable on the surface this is a result of too rapid drying-out. Plastered walls should not be forcibly dried. Use the warmth of a room with adequate ventilation, but don't play an electric fire directly onto the surface.

Plaster too hard to support decoration. Gypsum plasters sometimes set extremely hard on the surface. If this happens apply a solution consisting of one part of phosphoric acid by volume to eight of water, and leave for forty-eight hours for absorption to take place. Don't forget to add acid to water and not water to acid.

Plaster that is too dense or highly trowelled can be given a finishing coat of oil paint diluted with the same quantity of white spirit. This will adhere better on a hard surface than either plaster primer or undercoating. When dry, further coats of oil paint can be applied or a wallpaper hung on top.

Brown spots on distemper. Heavy condensation can cause the glue binder in distemper to leach out in the form of brown droplets. All you can do here is to try washing them off with warm water, not rubbing too hard or you will remove the distemper.

Staining and cracking of plaster over a buried copper pipe. This is very often seen and may be caused by (1) efflorescence in a new plaster filling, (2) sudden expansion and contraction of the copper, which is more violent than with a lead pipe, (3) a trembling pipe, (4) wet plaster corroding the metal (although copper does not rust, it will corrode).

Treat (1) as for efflorescence (page 20). Treat (2) by stripping the plaster and coating the pipe thickly with bituminous paint. While the paint is still wet, wrap a bandage of cloth round the pipe to take up movement and prevent the bitumen from bleeding through when you replaster. Or you can line the wall with paper to hide the cracks. Deal with (3) by stripping the plaster and anchoring the pipe more securely, and (4) by coating the pipe with bituminous paint and bandage.

Sulphiding. When a lead paint has been used, the presence of hydrogen sulphide in the atmosphere (perhaps from cosmetic sprays) can turn the surface grey or black. Paints containing cobalt driers and mercury preservatives have a similar effect, but to a lesser degree. Treat with hydrogen peroxide and repaint, using a lead-free paint. Paints with antimony in them sometimes turn an orange colour under the action of sulphur.

Fracturing of duplex wall covering. Duplex papers are generally hung over lining paper. If they become fractured – say, at the relief parts – the base paper will show through and discolour on exposure to light. Remedy: strip and repaper.

Staining of wallpaper over an oil-painted surface. Caused by condensation penetrating the paper and being stopped by a relatively hard surface. This softens up the paste. Remedy: strip and line the wall with polystyrene sheeting (see fire warning on page 33) before repapering; or use an embossed paper over a double lining.

Replastering

A woman friend of ours watched a professional plasterer at work on one room of her house. Then she replastered another room entirely on her own and made a perfect job – which proves that it is not so difficult as you might think.

Two important things have to be borne in mind. First, modern plasters set rapidly – an advantage insofar as you can get a job completed quickly, but a disadvantage in the fact that there is no time to waste. Each movement of the trowel must be deliberate and right first time. If you keep putting on and taking off you will get nowhere. Second, though the filling of holes and damaged patches presents no problems, the coating of a whole wall needs care and concentration. No amount of reading will make you a plasterer. You will have to watch a professional at work, noting particularly how he holds his float at an angle so that a cushion of air is pushed to the front, doing the job of levelling without rivelling.

Tell your builders' merchant what your job is and he will suggest the materials to use. Clean the wall substrate, wet it and apply the first or browning coat with about two or three parts of sand. Follow with a neat float coat and then a setting or finishing coat, lubricating the trowel with water as you proceed. Don't try to complete the job in one operation.

Criss-cross the first coats after they have started to set, using the edge of the trowel, to form a key. The thickness of the first coat should be about 10 mm. ($\frac{3}{8}$ in.), that of the float 10 to 15 mm. and setting coat 1 to 5 mm. ($\frac{1}{8}$ in.). Thickness can be gauged by putting dabs of plaster near the top and bottom of the wall at one side and tapping a short piece of lath well into each dab. Repeat at the other side, and plaster in between. After the wall has been completely floated, remove the laths and fill

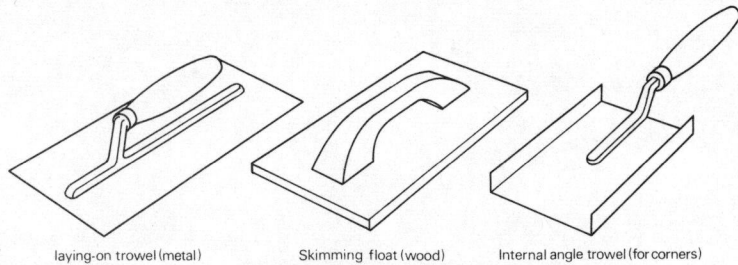

laying-on trowel (metal)   Skimming float (wood)   Internal angle trowel (for corners)

Fig. 5. Plasterer's trowels

the depressions. Give a final smooth over as the plaster is beginning to stiffen.

In addition to a hawk (Fig. 2) and small trowel for working behind pipes, the minimum of tools required will be a laying-on trowel, a skimming float and an internal angle trowel for corners (Fig. 5).

4
Floors
and
Ceilings

Underlay for Carpeting

Rough, uneven floorboards will cut a new carpet unless it is protected with an underlay. So it is more economic to buy a good underlay and an inexpensive carpet than have a good carpet and no underlay.

Some carpets have a built-in rubber backing which serves the purpose. Otherwise a sheet of felt, foam rubber or similar material will take up minor imperfections.

Similar care should be taken with linoleum. Even after punching nail-heads in, filling indentations with cellulose filler* and planing the edges of floorboards level, it is well to insert an underlay. One comprising cork granules on a bitumen backing does not cost much.

Plain-edged floorboards (those butted up to one another and not tongued and grooved) may shrink, leaving gaps; fill these with strips of wood of sufficient length to cover two adjoining joists so that they will not hammer through or tilt at one end. Plane the upper edges of the filling strips level with the surrounds. If it is impossible to get a perfectly level surface, cover the floor with hardboard – which is easy to cut and lay.

Squeaky Floorboards

It is humiliating and embarrassing when your floor responds to a visitor's tread with a cheeky squeak. This happens when one of the boards has worked loose, becomes depressed under body weight and springs back after the foot is removed. Its dry edges rub against the edges of the adjoining boards, or the board will ride up and down against the sides of the retaining nails.

Lift the floor covering and locate the faulty board. Make sure there are no underlying gas or water pipes or electric cables in the way and drive two more flooring nails in at a slant, one at each side of the board. Sometimes a board becomes loose by being taken up several times – perhaps to get at service pipes underneath – and there may be such a number of nail holes in it that it has become jagged or furred. In that case, insert screws instead of nails, counter-sinking their heads.

Carpets

Woven carpets contain a lot of loose fibres which are removed with repeated cleaning. Some manufacturers recommend hand brushing for the first month, after which a vacuum cleaner may be used. But this does not necessarily apply to tufted carpets because they have a backing which anchors the loops in position.

Give a carpet a quick go-over with a vacuum cleaner after a party rather than leave dirt to accumulate until the next time floor coverings are on the domestic cleaning programme. Ingrained grit can cause serious wear by cutting the fibres. A thorough cleaning with a good chemical cleaner once a year will restore the original colours. Leave the carpet to dry before moving the furniture back. If this is impossible, place grease-proof paper under the legs.

It will pay you to have your furniture legs fitted with good castors*, otherwise indentations will form. If patches are already flattened, bring them up with a damp cloth and hot iron.

The modern fitting of a wall-to-wall carpet consists of grippers – strips of wood or metal with spikes arranged at an angle. The carpet is forced over these to hold it in place, a method far superior to the old idea of using tacks.

Naturally a carpet will wear more between door and fireplace and, to a lesser extent, between door and window. Wear can be evened out by turning; but a fitted carpet cannot be turned unless it is plain or has a nondescript pattern and is cut into sections as is indicated in Fig. 6A. Portion (a) is square and can be turned three times. Portions (b) and (c) are

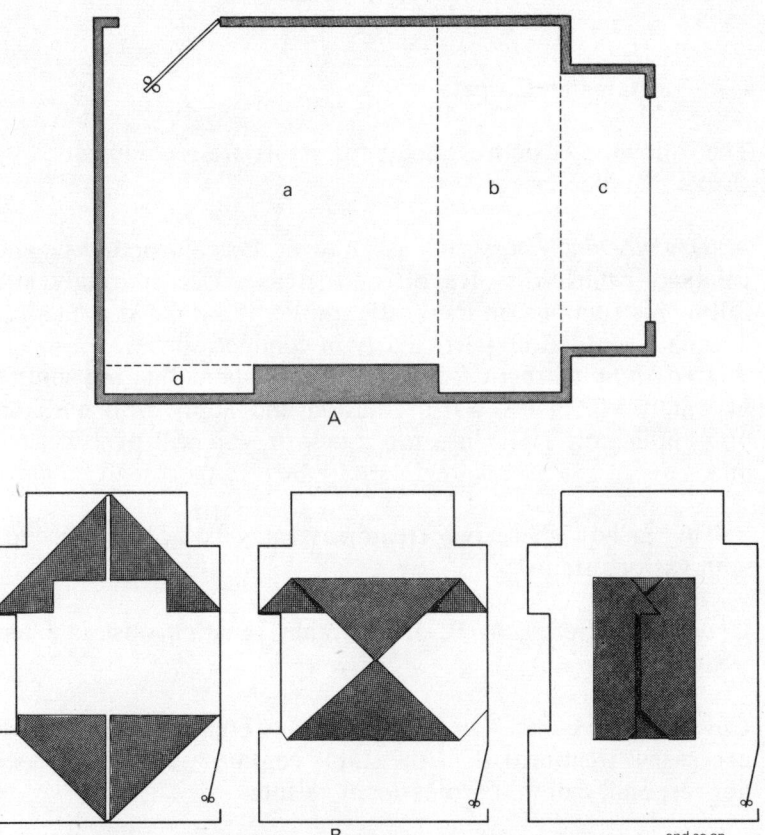

Fig. 6. A – Fitted carpet cut in sections for turning. B – How to fold up a fitted carpet

rectangular and can be turned once. There is little wear on (d) and so this part does not require turning. If this idea is adopted, some form of anchoring will have to be devised, such as jointing tape at the edges.

A hearth rug pays for itself if only because it takes excessive heel wear from visitors sitting by your fireside.

Don't roll a fitted carpet to clear the floor ready for decorating a room. Fold it corner to corner diagonally, then again corner to corner as is shown in Fig. 6B, and it will fall back in its exact position when you wish to relay it.

Stair carpets are dealt with in Chapter 9.

Stains on Carpets

The following basic treatments for stains are recommended by carpet manufacturers:

A. *Dry cleaning fluids* such as Thawpit, Perchloroethylene and Inhibisol which dissolve oil and grease. Use sparingly and follow instructions on the bottle implicitly. Make sure there is adequate ventilation, particularly in confined spaces.
B. *Dry Foam Carpet Cleaner* for use on stains that are soluble in water. Mix a lukewarm solution and apply with a shampoo applicator. Don't use too much or you will over-wet the pile.

This is how these two treatments may be applied to cope with various stains:

Chocolate: Treatment B. If the stain remains obstinate use treatment A.

Cosmetics (creams, lotions, lipsticks): Treatment A and, if necessary, treatment B. If the stains contain a dye which does not respond, call in a professional cleaner.

Drinks – alcoholic (beers, wines, spirits): Mop up and apply treatment B.

Drinks – non-alcoholic (cocoa, coffee, soft drinks, fruit juice): Treatment B. You may also have to use methylated spirit.

Tea: Treatment B followed by treatment A if necessary.

Milk: The same as for tea.

Nail varnish: Sponge with nail varnish remover or amylacetate.

Paint, oil, grease, tar: Treatment A followed by treatment B.

Rust: Treatment A. You may also have to apply a *small quantity* of a rust remover.

Shoe polish: Treatment A. If stain persists, sponge with methylated spirit.

Soot: Vacuum gently. Then follow with treatment B and, when dry, by treatment A.

Ink: Blot immediately. Dab with warm milk and finish off with treatment B. For ball-point ink stains use methylated spirit to which has been added a small amount of white vinegar. Blot continuously. Finish off with treatment B.

Urine and animal upsets: Treatment B, adding one part of white vinegar to three of the cleaner. Rinse and mop several times with water. Apply a thick pad of white blotting paper, leaving the pile no more than damp. Support the damp patch above the level of the floor with a piece of wood so that it dries quickly.

Wax: Treatment A.

Floor Tiles

Make sure that gas and water pipes, electricity cables and so on, which may run underneath the floor, are in good order. There is no fun in having to rip up a permanently tiled floor too soon after it is laid.

Some tiles are made to be laid with a special adhesive (recommended by the manufacturer). Others are self-adhesive.

To lay the first kind find the centre of each of the longest opposing sides of the room and rough-nail chalked string across the room at these points, twanging it so that it leaves a line on the floor. The centre of this line will be the centre of the room. Place a tile with one corner just covering this centre point, and one edge just covering the line. Place a straight board up to the adjacent edge of the tile, remove the tile and draw a chalk mark on the floor, following through until you reach the two shortest sides of the room (Fig. 7A).

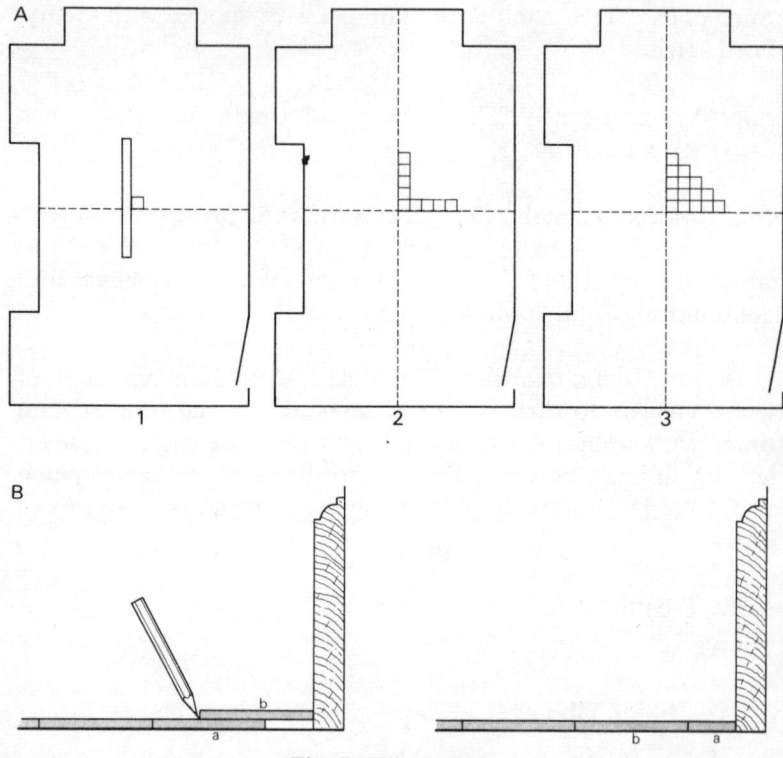

Fig. 7. Tiling a floor

Spread adhesive (the kind prescribed by the tile manufacturer) along one side of one line for approximately half its length. Lay the tiles along this part aligning the chalk mark. Carry on in a similar way along the line running at right-angles. Stick tiles in between the right-angled gap thus formed and continue until the whole of that quarter is completed before attending to the other quarters in turn.

When approaching the edges of the room, lay the penultimate tile (a) in position without adhesive (Fig. 7B). Stand another tile (b) on top so that it butts onto the wall or skirting board. Mark the extent of the overlap of (b) over (a). Cut (a) and remove the overlapped part of (a). Move (b) next to the last laid tile and the remaining part of (a) will abut the wall.

Vinyl Flooring

Whereas linoleum spreads with walking over – that is why final trimming has to be delayed for some weeks after laying– continuous vinyl floor covering tends to shrink, and provision should be made for that when it is first put down.

Continuous and tiled vinyl can be kept in good order by merely sweeping and mopping over once a day to remove surface grit. Don't use detergents or polishes not specifically formulated for the purpose as they may disrupt the surface. Consult the manufacturer's literature on this point. On no account use abrasive cleaners or wirewool.

To remove a damaged tile for replacement, run a sharp knife around its edges to break the adhesive film, lift a corner and try and peel it off. Sometimes cutting the faulty tile into small pieces is more effective. If this does not do the job, lay a thin sheet of metal, no larger than the tile, over it and apply a hot domestic iron. Take care not to heat up surrounding tiles or they may blister. Scrape old adhesive from the sub-floor, applying heat if necessary. Where there is an underlay, parts of it may come away with the tile; if this happens, you will have to make it good before laying a fresh tile.

A word of warning. When laying linoleum or vinyl floor covering over a floor that you have treated with wood preservative to get rid of woodworm, insert polythene sheeting underneath, or the covering may wrinkle. After the preservative has been allowed to soak well in for some weeks, the danger is not so great with linoleum, but vinyl may still be affected.

Ceilings

Lath and plaster ceilings crack through shrinkage, subsidence of the building structure, broken laths or by joists not being strong enough to take a wide span; that is to say, footsteps overhead may cause them to 'spring'.

Shrinkage always happens with a new house. The finest of resulting hair cracks can quickly be filled with emulsion paint, and ceiling paper will 'bridge' over them. Wide cracks should be undercut, wetted and stopped up proud, using two applications of a cellulose filler*. When dry, sand level with the surrounding parts.

Cracks whose width is between hair cracks and big ones — that is to say, they are too narrow to undercut and too wide to fill with paint — can be patched up by mixing a little filler to a creamy consistency and painting it into the crack with a fine brush. While it is still wet, knife over some more filler mixed to the usual mustard consistency, and press it in firmly. The thick material will follow the thinner into the crack. Leave proud and sand level when dry.

Subsidence may cause one side of a crack to be lower than the other and this will lead to a noticeably uneven ceiling if the filler is just knifed in and smoothed over. Test whether the plaster is firm by tapping with the handle of a trowel; if it sounds hollow, hack away the plaster until you reach a firm edge. You can tell whether the edges of the plaster are true by placing a straight board over it. If the discrepancy is extreme, cut away more plaster so that the wave in the ceiling, after filling, will be spread over a wider area and will not be so obvious.

Broken laths can be replaced after chipping away plaster from the affected area. A subsequent patching up will be easily within the ability of a careful do-it-yourselfer.

Weak joists will need reinforcing if it is not feasible to lessen the traffic overhead. One way of doing this is to lift the floorboards in the room above and nail on a plank of wood to the side of each joist; but if the whip is excessive, it would be better to call in a builder.

Completely replastering a ceiling is more difficult than replastering a wall and may be beyond the abilities of most amateurs. But nailing up plasterboard or insulating board or $\frac{1}{8}$ in. (3·2 mm.) standard hardboard with non-ferrous nails can easily be done. You may need to nail through old friable plaster. Find where the joists are by measuring the distance from the wall of a line of exposed flooring nail-heads in the room above, and transfer this measurement to the ceiling below. Now measure the distance between one row of nail-heads to the next to find the distance between the joists; this will be in the neighbourhood of 350 to 400 mm. (14 to 16 in.).

Joins between the ceiling sheets are filled by tapering the edges. Some sheets are sold already tapered. Brush in a thinned coat of plaster, insert a length of scrim and plaster a proud filling on top which can be sanded level when dry (Fig. 8).

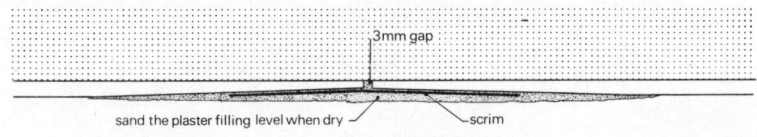

sand the plaster filling level when dry /   ＼scrim

Fig. 8. Dry ceiling join

Unfortunately, the joins will always form a weak point where cracks may develop. In the author's opinion it is better to cut the sheets to a design that will make the most economic use of the board without giving a patched-up effect. When these pieces are nailed up, thin wooden or plastic moulding strips may be nailed or stuck over the joins to form a decorated ceiling.

Polystyrene

Polystyrene has become suspect on account of fire hazards. Indeed, some town councils will not allow even the self-extinguishing grades in their houses.

This is a great pity because polystyrene is excellent for disguising a ceiling that, even though clean and firm, has an uneven surface. The material will also act as an insulator, reducing condensation. It will take ceiling paper or it can be painted over with emulsion paint. Oil paint will disrupt the surface; what is worse, it constitutes an added fire hazard.

As you will be working overhead, cut the sheets into smallish sections for ease of handling. A simpler way is to stick on polystyrene tiles, following the procedure already described for laying tiled floors (page 30). Tiles with attractive printed designs are available. The snag with many of these is that, when they get discoloured, freshening up with emulsion paint will obliterate the pattern. Some brands are treated with a dirt-repellent chemical and can be sponged over with warm water.

You can buy fire-retardant tiles and decorate them with fire-retardant emulsion*. The adhesive should be spread all over the backs of the tiles and not in blobs, as is customary.

5
Fireplaces

Smoky Chimney

Air expands on being heated – which means that less warm than cool air will be required to fill a given space. Warm air is therefore lighter in weight than cool air and so tends to rise.

A flue makes use of this principle. Air is heated by the flames of a fire and rises up the chimney carrying smoke and fumes with it. That is what it should do – but sometimes it doesn't. If it doesn't, these are the faults to look for:

Dirty chimney. The remedy here is obvious – get it swept.

Obstruction in the chimney, such as a misplaced brick or, if the fire has not been used for some time, a bird's nest. Remedy – get the sweep to rod out the obstruction.

Lack of air supply. Naturally, if air is being sucked up the chimney, more air must enter the room to replace it. A fault of the modern craze for sealing doors, bottoms of skirting boards and door surrounds is that, if carried to excess, a fresh supply of air is excluded and the fire just won't burn. One way out of the difficulty is to have a vent in the floor at each side of the hearth through which air can enter from under the floorboards without causing a draught. A mere hole in the floor would do. Or you can buy fittings which can be secured to the floor and are operated by a valve allowing air to enter but not to get out. A similar fitting can be inserted into an inside opposing wall higher up where it will not cause draughts – which is useful when there is a solid floor.

The fireplaces we have dealt with are those that draw their air supply from above floor level. There is another kind which gets its supply from underfloor draught*. This burns even if the room is exceedingly well sealed; and an additional advantage is that, to replace the air sucked up from underneath the floor-boards, fresh air enters through the air bricks from outside – ensuring an under-floor circulation which is the best preventative against dry rot.

Cold chimney. When a fire has not been lit for some time the chimney lining gets cold. Warm air rising from a newly lit fire will rapidly cool as it contacts the lining, causing smoke to rise half-way up and then, becoming heavier, to drop, bringing clouds of smoke and fumes into the room. If this occurs, all you can do is wait until the chimney warms up – which will not take long – and try to reduce the down draught in the meantime by manipulating doors and windows. As every fireplace has its eccentricities you will have to experiment with each room to see what happens.

Smoking due to a chilled chimney mostly takes place when the stack is built on an outside wall exposed to wind, and also to rain soaking the bricks. In evaporating, the water will chill the stack. In addition to less exposure to weather when a chimney is built on an inside wall, there will be less loss of heat.

The bricks of a chimney above roof level may be old and porous. To prevent their getting too damp and cold give the outside two applications of a silicone waterproofing solution. This will not be effective, however, if the jointing between the bricks has decayed. The only remedy here is repointing (see Chapter 2). When examining the brickwork check that the flaunching (mortar seal between chimney pot and stack) and the oversailing course are sound. The object of the oversailing course is to throw rain clear of the bricks underneath (see Fig. 1).

If any of these parts needs attention you will have to call in a builder who may be able to cure the trouble by inserting a flexible flue liner. A builder should most certainly be consulted if the stack leans over to one side. Imagine what will happen if a high wind blows it down!

Chimneys that have remained sound for years often develop a tilt after an open grate has been discarded for a slow combustion stove – perhaps because the area in which the house is situated has been made a smokeless zone. Coke, anthracite and patent fuels used in such stoves may give forth more sulphurous fumes than ordinary coal; in any case the fumes are not expelled so quickly, which means that they have a better chance of attacking the brickwork if there is no flue liner to protect it. Sometimes the fault may be cured by inserting an air brick in a boiler chimney near the ceiling, through which air is sucked in to dilute damp poisonous gases and lessen the possibility of condensation.

Badly designed fireplace. Measure the height between the top of the front of the grate and the lintel (top of the fireplace). This should not be much more than 450 mm. (18 in.) for the usual size of room. If it is, experiment with a sheet of cardboard held in front, raising or lowering it after a fire has been lit; and when you have got it right, fix a cowl or sheet of metal, such as burnished copper or aluminium, permanently in position. An undesirable increase in height often occurs when a modern sunken fire has been installed in place of an old-type barred grate.

At the same time, make sure that the surface of the throat (see Fig. 9A) is smooth, because projections can deflect smoke downwards. If the throat is too large, suction may be sluggish; and its length should be 200 to 250 mm. (8 to 10 in.). Here you may have to install an adjustable throat restrictor. You can bend a sheet of metal to fit the throat, curving the upper edge inwards as a first experiment.

Badly designed chimney. If, after checking and correcting all these points, you still get a smoky room, go into the garden and compare the height of your chimney with the height of the ridge of the roof and with neighbouring buildings and trees. If it is much lower, eddies of air will form at the top of the stack and prevent the escape of smoke (Fig. 9B). The most certain way of correcting the effect of these eddies is to increase the height of the chimney stack. Sometimes you can put the fault

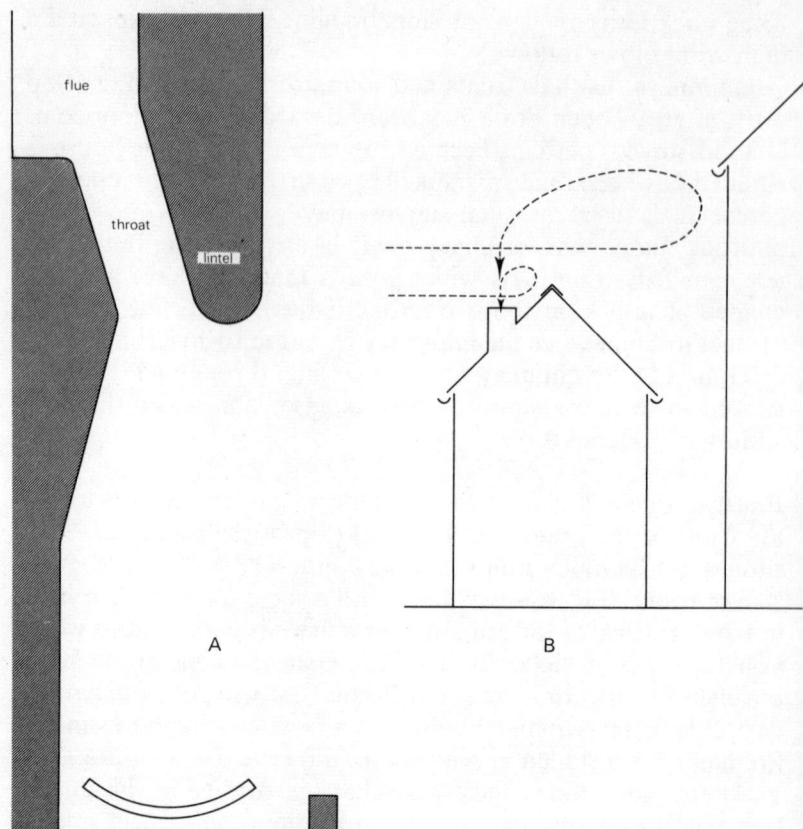

Fig. 9. A – Parts of a chimney. B – Excessively low chimney

right by fitting a cowl, but any old cowl will not do. Seek professional advice before spending your money.

A country house at the foot of a mountain often suffers from smoky chimneys when wind is blowing from the direction of the mountain. In this case, air is deflected over the top to sweep down on the chimney stack.

Cracked Fireback

Leaving cracks in the back of a fireplace is dangerous. Cut them out and patch up with fireclay* once a year, after you finished with winter fires. New firebacks can be bought in sections to fit the standard widths of fires.

Open fires of the all-night type should be completely sealed around the hearth and sides to ensure proper slow burning when the front is closed. Fire cement on its own will soon crack, so caulk the gaps first with asbestos cord.

Cracked Hearth

What causes the crack one often sees on a hearth running from the back of the centre of a fireplace?

It is expansion and contraction of the cement mortar holding the tiles; and the fault will continue unless a weaker mortar – say, one part by volume of cement, five parts of sand and one of lime – is used. Even then, results are not assured. Another method, which also cannot be guaranteed, is to place a sheet of heat-resisting asbestos * on the base and fix the tiles with a tile cement on top.

If individual tiles become damaged it will be almost impossible to chip them out without also loosening those adjacent; and the only remedy is to smash the whole hearth with a cold chisel and hammer and lay new ones. With an old-fashioned fireplace having a character you do not wish to destroy, you will find it difficult to buy tiles to match those of the surrounds – unless you can get them second-hand from a demolition contractor.

One way out – the only one we can suggest, though it may be unpopular – is to discard tiles altogether and lay a mortar hearth comprising one part of cement and four of sand by volume. This will look an objectionable grey, but it can be made and kept white by periodically running over with pipe-clay, as our grandmothers used to do.

If you have difficulty in getting pipeclay make your own hearth paint by mixing one part by volume of glue size to about fifteen parts of whiting, with sufficient water to give it a creamy consistency, and brush it on. This will take only a few minutes and about half an hour to dry. When it becomes blackened by falling coals, a rub over with a wet cloth will dissolve the glue and spread the surrounding white to cover the black. After two or three wipings over with a wet cloth, what is left of the coating will have to be washed off – an easy matter – and renewed.

You can mix up a quantity of this paint in advance to last a considerable time. If you don't want to go to the trouble you can use non-washable size-bound distemper * instead. This does not, however, spread so easily under the action of a wet cloth.

Don't attempt to use an oil paint because the intense heat immediately in front of the fire will cause blistering and a horrible smell. Don't use emulsion paint either, because it will discolour.

Stained and Cracked Chimney Breast

Before the advent of the television set, the focal point of a room was the fireplace. To a great extent it still is. What more annoying a spectacle can there be than a breast that is cracked through heat from the fire or stained through exuding wet soot?

If the cracks are bad, undercut and fill them, and paper the breast with an embossed paper, hanging a lining paper underneath if the embossed paper is heavy. This will 'give' with any further expansion and contraction. Fine cracks need not be filled; the paper will bridge over them.

If there are only a few stains here and there touch them in with aluminium primer sealer.

6
Doors

Unsticking

What makes a door stick?

Swollen wood or misplaced hinges perhaps; or structural subsidence causing the case (surrounding framework) to drop.

When a door does not close properly, the first thing the average paterfamilias does is to bring out his plane and go to work on the edges. Later the wood dries out, shrinks, and a wide gap is left to grin back at him. It requires only a few minutes to take something off but it is a very big job to add something on; so, before starting to cure the sticking, try to trace its cause.

Swollen joints, the result of damp, can be cured only by improving and maintaining heat. Inevitably a new door is slightly damp, maybe because the timber from which it is made is not seasoned as thoroughly as it should be or, in the case of a new house, because the door has been stored in the open before assembly. When first painting a new door, leave the top edge bare and, in time, entrapped moisture will run along the grain of the wood, reach the exposed parts and evaporate. After the wood is dry, later repaints can include the top edge. It is always easier to dust painted than unpainted wood.

If the door sticks at the top vertical edge, stand back and see if there is an even tolerance all round. Suppose there is a wide gap at the hanging side of the top edge and it decreases to nothing at the opening side of the top edge, then the setting of the hinges will be at fault. This is shown in an extremely exaggerated form in Fig. 10A, and can be remedied by taking off the door and deepening the rebate into which the butt of the hinge is sunk, by using a chisel. The top hinge will then be set farther into the door-case. Take very little wood off at a time; if too much is removed you will find that the top hanging edge will stick (Fig. 10B).

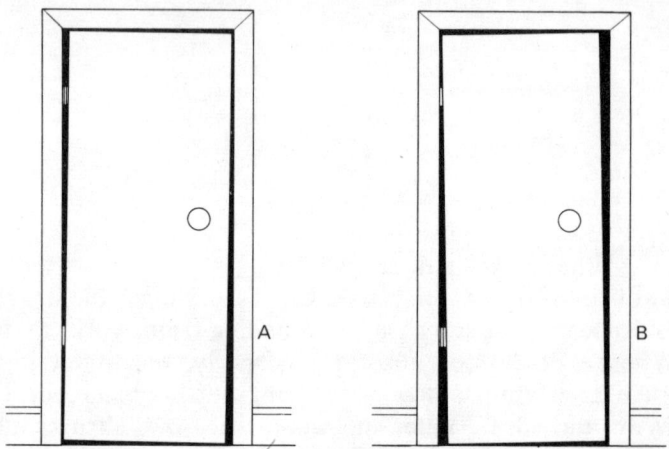

Fig. 10. Sticking doors. A – Top hinge requires resetting farther into the doorcase. B – Top hinge requires packing out.

In the event of your making such a mistake, or maybe the door requires bringing out from the top hanging side because of subsidence or other reasons, pack thin card between the butt of the hinge and the recess. As there is no formula for this adjustment, you will just have to do the job by trial and error.

Don't cut the bottom of an otherwise perfectly fitting door to allow it to clear a centrally placed square of carpet. Fit rising-butt hinges which will lift the door on opening. As the rising motion will begin when the door starts to open, the top edge on the hanging side will foul the lintel of the case. Whittle some wood off – again doing the job little by little and by trial and error, using judgement. Where there is a fitted carpet, you may of course *have* to cut the bottom of the door.

Draught is prevented from entering a room at the sides and top of a door by the stop, a narrow strip of wood nailed to the case (Fig. 11). A twisted door will not meet this stop evenly all round, and plastic foam draught excluder may be stuck on to fill the gap. This is effective only with some doors. When a door meets the stop at the bottom vertical edge and not at the top, the foam will have to be tapered. This is difficult. Sticking on a strip at the widest part and cutting it off square will mean that a smaller tapered gap is still left in the middle.

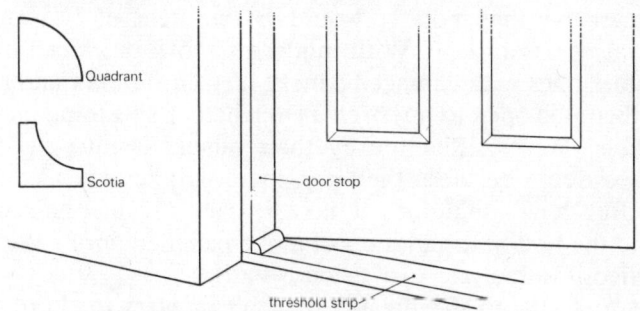

Fig. 11. Threshold draught strip

Far better to take off the stop and reset it to conform to the twist of the door when it is closed.

There is no stop at the bottom of a door-case and it is here that most draught enters. You can fit one by screwing a strip of wood to the floor between the side vertical stops, of width equal to them and thickness of about 9 mm. ($\frac{3}{8}$ in.). Place the strip in position with the door closed and press it firmly into the bottom of the door before securing permanently with one screw in the centre and one at each side.

Tiled floors will have to be bored to take screws, and the holes filled with asbestos filler. This may interfere with the sub-floor damp-proof course. So a better way is to attach the strip to the side stops with quadrant or scotia moulding as is shown in Fig. 11.

If there is a danger of elderly or very young people tripping over this 'threshold strip', as it might be called, you will have to

fit one of the patent draught excluders which automatically lift
when a door is opened and drop when closed.

Sheathing

Before blindly following the fashion for covering a panelled
door with hardboard, think whether this is desirable and in
keeping with the period of the room.

Sixty years ago seasoned timber would be brought into a
house in the course of building, and a panelled door made by a
carpenter on the spot. It would be an item of beauty and
covering it a sacrilege. With modern factory-produced doors,
and older ones with damaged panels, it is a different matter. But
even then it is open to question as to whether sheathing is really
desirable. Wives often jockey their husbands into sheathing
panelled doors because, they say, there will be fewer ledges to
dust. But how long does it take to run a camel-hair brush
around the bottom mouldings of a five-panelled door? We have
just tried it ourselves − 11 seconds flat!

If you decide to sheathe a door you can carry the hardboard
right to the edges on the opening side; but on the closing side
the stops will be in the way, necessitating removing them and
resetting farther back. A simpler way of getting over this difficulty is to pin the sheet of hardboard 25 mm. (1 in.) or so short
of the top, bottom and sides, covering the edges with ornamental wooden moulding.

Paint the sheathing with undercoat and finishing coat of an
alkyd resin or polyurethane paint over a primer consisting of
emulsion paint thinned with the same quantity of water. Or it
can be covered with self-adhesive vinyl sheeting *.

Painting Doors

These are the quickest and most effective procedures for door
painting:

Flush sheathed doors. Lay on and brush out paint over the
top third of the door and lay off lightly with the tips of the

bristles in a downward direction. Lay off the middle third in an upward direction into the band of previously applied wet paint. In a similar way, lay off the bottom third upwards (Fig. 12A).

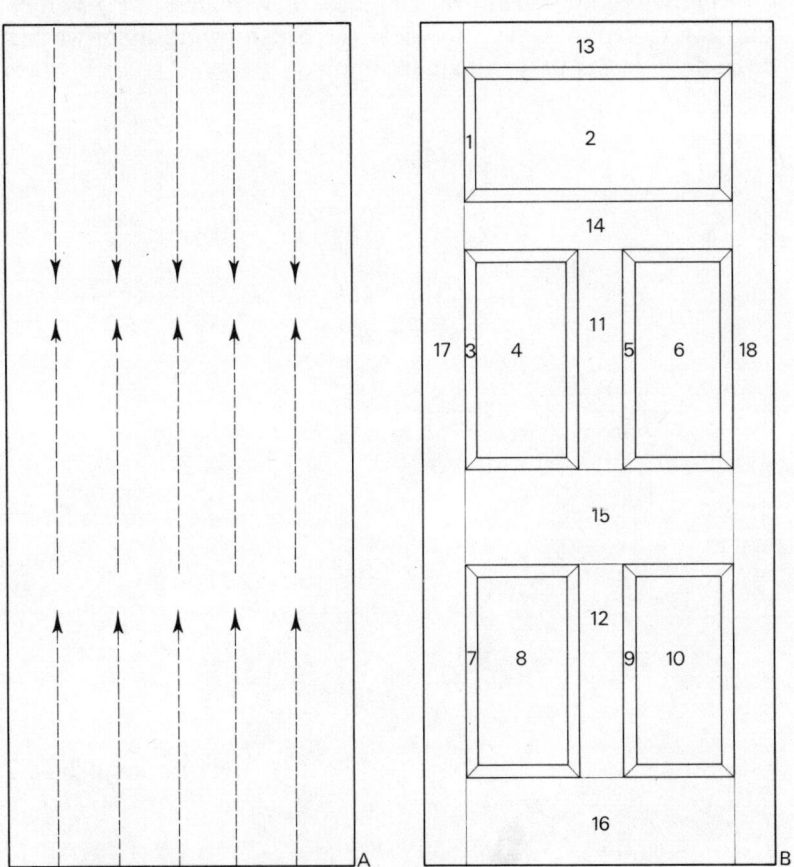

Fig. 12. A – Procedure for laying off paint on a sheathed door. B – Procedure for painting panelled door: 1 to 10 – mouldings and panels; 11 and 12 – muntins; 13 to 16 – cross rails; 17 and 18 – stiles

Panelled doors. Paint mouldings and panels first, then the muntins, then cross rails, then stiles – in each case picking up overlaps of paint and laying off in the direction of the grain of the wood (Fig. 12B).

These procedures apply to all coats – priming, undercoating and finishing. Use wood primer for wood, emulsion paint thinned with the same quantity of water for hardboard, and for heat-resisting asbestos lining*.

Remove door furniture (handles, key plates, etc.) before starting to paint. Trying to wield the brush round them wastes time and results in an amateurish job.

7
Windows

Sliding sash windows (those that open by pulling up and down) keep out weather better than do casement windows (those hinged like a door). Some windows are hinged at the top; others hinge in the centre and can be twisted round or lifted out for ease of cleaning. Picture windows consist of an expanse of glass covering a large portion of one side of a room. Louvre windows* look something like transparent venetian blinds, the individual panes opening and closing on a similar principle.

Window sashes are generally of wood or metal. The former are liable to rot and the latter to rust unless made of aluminium. Though plastic sashes neither rot nor rust, they are not too popular − possibly on account of the difficulty of painting over them if a colour change is desired.

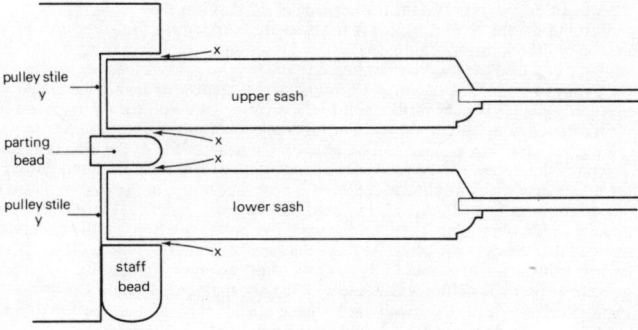

Fig. 13. Causes of a sash window sticking

Wooden casement windows are liable to stick through expansion during wet weather and may be put right by following the same procedure as for doors (Chapter 6). Sliding sash windows will also stick through expansion; but the trouble is more often due to accumulations of paint between sash stile and beading (Fig. 13 at (x)), or too thick a coat of paint being on the pulley stiles (y). You can remove excess paint with a chemical paint remover* and by scraping while the sash is out for renewal of sashcord. Don't use a blow-lamp when the sash is in place or you will almost certainly crack the glass.

Fig. 14. Mending sash cord

1. Open the top sash and cut the four exposed cords near the sashes with a sharp knife or hack-saw. Hold each cord while you are cutting and lower it gently, otherwise the weight concealed behind the pulley stile will fall heavily.

2. Prise out one side staff bead by inserting a blunt broad chisel in the middle. Lever the chisel sufficiently to grasp the bead and pull it out. When the three nails with which it is secured are exposed it can be removed with ease. Lift out the lower sash and take off what is left of the old cord – nailed in a groove on each side. You may also have to remove the other side staff bead before the sash will come out. There is no need to touch top and bottom staff beads.

3. Prise out parting beads on each side with a blunt chisel (they are not as a rule secured by nails). Remove the lower sash. Prise out pocket pieces (generally secured by a nail at the top and a lip of wood at the bottom). Put your hand in the pockets thus exposed and lift out the lower sash weights. You will now feel a loose dividing lath in the pocket; pull this aside and lift out the upper sash weights. Untie cords attached to the weights.

4. Tie one end of a piece of thread to a 'mouse' (a nut or screw or short length of metal chain small enough to ride over the pulley) and the other end to a hank of new sash cord.

5. Insert the 'mouse' over pulley (a) and allow it to drop until you can pull it out of pocket (y), drawing the cord with it. Insert the 'mouse' over pulley (b) and draw through pocket (z). Insert the 'mouse' over pulley (c) and draw through pocket (y). Insert the 'mouse' over pulley (d) and draw through pocket (z). Detach thread from the sash cord and tie the same end of the cord to a sash weight, making sure that no free ends are hanging loose to interfere with its passage up and down. Place the weight in pocket (z) on the farther side of the dividing lath.

6. Pull the weight up to the top and measure three-quarters of the way down from the top of the window opening, cut the cord there and exert your strength to stretch the cord and firm the knot connecting it to the weight. Drive a wooden wedge over the pulley to keep it in position. Tie the end of the uncut cord to another weight and place in pocket (y) on the farther side of the dividing lath. Pull tightly to the top and wedge in position. Measure three-quarters way down and cut. Repeat over pulleys (b) and (a), this time placing the weights on the nearer side of the dividing lath.

7. Attach the free end of the cord passing over pulley (d) to the right-hand groove of the upper sash with one clout nail driven in near the bottom of the groove. Take out the wedge in pulley (d). Attach the cord passing over pulley (c) to the left-hand groove with a clout nail. Take out the wedge in pulley (c). Replace the upper sash and test that it works properly. Remove the sash and insert two more clout nails on each side, near the first ones at the bottom of the grooves. Replace the upper sash permanently. Replace the pocket pieces. Replace the parting beads. Carry out the same procedure with the lower sash whose cords will ride over pulleys (b) and (a). Replace the staff bead and punch in the nail heads below the surface, filling in with putty.

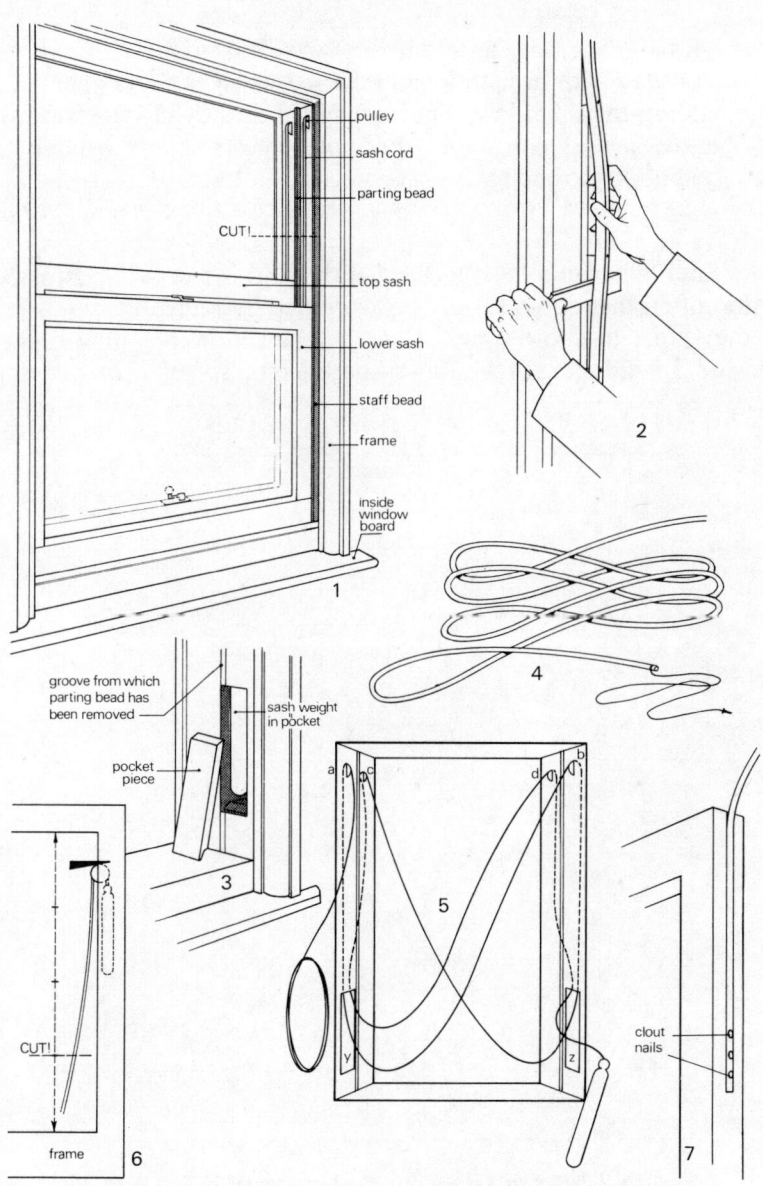

pulley

sash cord

parting bead

CUT!

top sash

lower sash

staff bead

frame

inside
window
board

1

2

groove from which
parting bead has
been removed

sash weight
in pocket

pocket
piece

3

4

a   c   d   b

5

y   z

clout
nails

CUT!

frame

6

7

Sashcords

Mrs —— was admitted to the Borough Hospital on Tuesday with broken fingers caused when she was opening a sliding-sash window. The cords broke, allowing the window to drop and entrapping her until her screams brought a neighbour to the rescue.

– Local newspaper

Such accidents happen frequently, and it cannot be stressed too often that cords should be examined periodically and, when they start to show signs of wear, renewed before they break. Modern sliding sash windows operate on a spring principle and

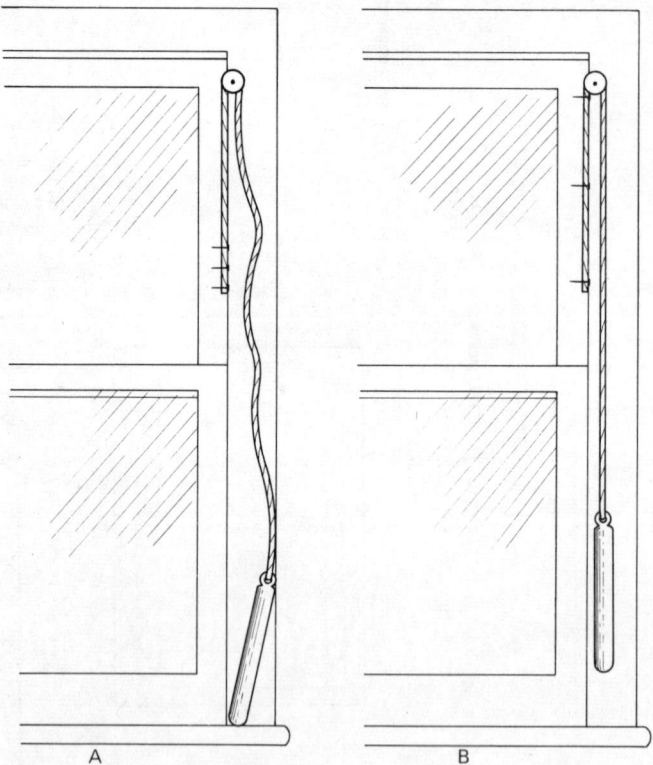

A   B

Fig. 15. Causes of sashes not closing properly. A – Sash cord too long. B – Cord nailed too high in sash groove, allowing insufficient length to ride over pulleys

no cords are involved, but the vast majority are balanced with compensating weights hidden behind pulley stiles.

If one cord is weak or broken, don't just attend to this, renew all four, because it will not be long before the others go, and it is difficult to remove a sash without marring the decoration. The instructions in Fig. 14 (1–7) show the quickest way to do the job and the one most economical on sash cord – which is obtainable from a hardware merchant and should be of the waxed variety for long life.

If the top sash will not close properly after being tested, the fault will be due to one of two reasons. The cords may be too long so that the weights rest on the bottom of the pocket before the sash reaches the top (Fig. 15A). When cutting is done at the three-quarters mark indicated in diagram 6 of Fig. 14, this seldom happens; if it does, lift out the sashes and correct the error. Or it may be that the clout nails holding the cord to the sash have been driven in too high up in the grooves, allowing insufficient length of cord to ride over the pulleys (Fig. 15B).

That is why only one clout nail is suggested when testing; it can quickly be pulled out and an adjustment made.

Never paint a sash cord. Pull it clear with one hand and pass the paint brush underneath. Paint stiffens the fibres which will snap off when passing over the pulley, so weakening the whole cord.

Replacing Broken Panes

To take out a broken pane, work from the outside: find the weakest part of the putty fillet holding the pane in its rebate (generally on the bottom rail) and chip it away. Hold the knife against the broken end of sound putty and tap its back with a hammer to remove the remainder, protecting the hands with gloves and pulling out fragments of broken glass as you go.

Clean the rebate by scraping and sanding.

Measure the space to be occupied by the new pane and deduct about 4 mm. ($\frac{1}{8}$ in.) from its depth and the same from its width, allowing for 2 mm. ($\frac{1}{16}$ in.) tolerance all round. Before ordering the glass to this measurement from a glass merchant, it is just as well to check that the sash is perfectly rectangular.

To do this, measure from the top left-hand corner to the bottom right-hand corner, and from the top right corner to the bottom left corner. If these two measurements, (a)–(b) and (c)–(d) (see Fig. 16A), are the same, you are all right. If not, you will have to cut a paper pattern of the opening.

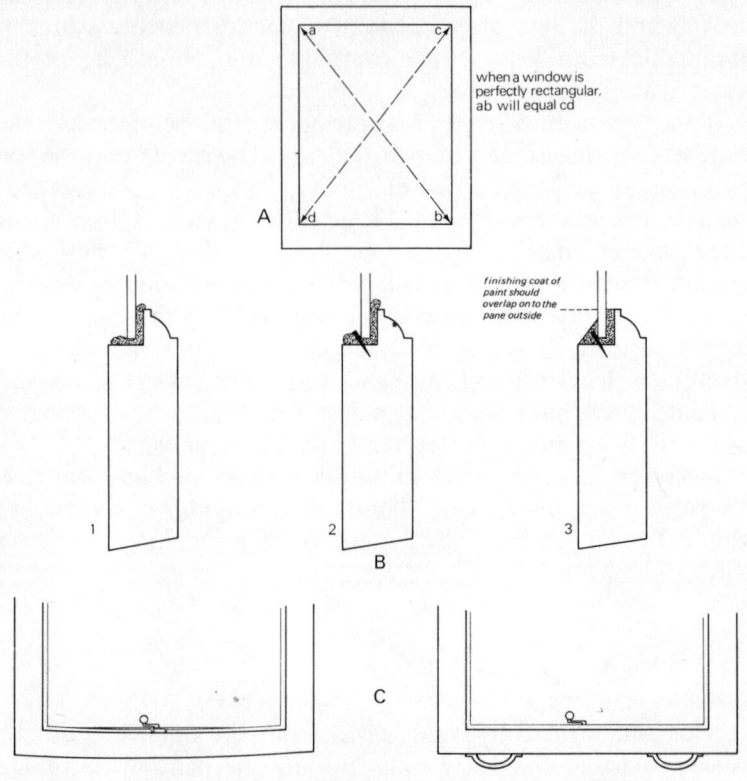

Fig. 16. Glazing. A – Checking that sash is perfectly rectangular. B – Pane and window frame in cross-section: (1) new pane pressed into putty; (2) pane secured with brad; (3) more putty applied and knifed off. C – Weak window frame with handles attached

Apply a coat of wood primer over the bare rebate to prevent too much oil being soaked up from the putty. When dry, knead a little putty in the palm of your hand, spread a thin layer in the rebate all round and press in the new pane to 1 or 2 mm. ($\frac{1}{32}$ in.) from the wood. Secure this in position with glazing brads (small tacks without heads) as you would when backing a picture in a frame. For a smallish window, two brads are sufficient for the top, two for the bottom and three on each side. Larger windows will require more in proportion. The safest way to knock in brads without breaking the glass is to allow the head of the tack hammer to glide over the pane without leaving the surface.

Apply more putty to the outside, squeezing it well in and knifing off with a putty knife at an angle so that the top of the angle comes about 3 or 4 mm. ($\frac{1}{8}$ in.) below the top of the rebate which you will be able to see through the glass. This space will be put to use when you paint the sash. By taking the finishing coats of paint (not primer or undercoat which do not adhere to glass all that well) onto the glass slightly all round you will seal the top edge of the putty and prevent rain from entering behind. If this film of paint is brought level with the top of the rebate you will have a neat, professional-looking job. Scrape exuding putty from the inside of the pane.

These three steps are shown in Fig. 16B.

Neat and professional ...? Well, it may hardly be that when you make your first attempt at glazing. Do not despair, however, if your putty fillet shows slight waviness. You will be only too aware of imperfections when working close to it; but after the job has been painted, other people will not notice the fault provided it is not too pronounced. You will become more proficient with practice, particularly if you watch professional glaziers at work, and note how they palm a ball of kneaded putty and 'pay' it out between first finger and thumb.

Leave the new putty for at least a week and not more than a month before painting it in dry weather, or six weeks in humid conditions, or wrinkling will result.

Metal windows require a special putty which, to a degree, is rust inhibiting and takes up the considerable expansion and contraction changes to which metal is subject. Use clips to hold the pane on metal sashes, not glazing brads.

Louvre window panes (called blades) of the 'Louvre King' type* are replaced in the same way as they are put in, though you may have to open the blade holder clips slightly to allow the new blade to be inserted.

Corroded Metal Windows

Zinc chromate, red lead and zinc-rich primers are rust-inhibiting. That is to say, they prevent clean metal from corroding and, if corrosion has started, they hinder it from spreading. Of the three, we prefer zinc chromate primer because it is safest to use and brushes on smoothly. It should be applied over new steel and aluminium. Galvanised iron is iron coated with zinc, and *new* zinc (revealed by its bright silveriness) requires calcium plumbate primer. Zinc chromate, which is cheaper, will do for old weathered zinc (revealed by its dull grey colour).

Suppose you have a steel window which has rusted through neglect of a past owner of your house, or a galvanised iron one, the zinc coating of which has worn or become chipped, exposing parts of bare rusted iron. First scrape the red patches and rub them with emery cloth. This will get rid of the bulk of the rust; but microscopic particles may still be left behind which will tend to spread under a new paint film. One of three courses is open to you:

(1) Neutralise the remaining rust and reprime immediately or rust will re-form very quickly.

(2) Turn the iron oxide (rust) into phosphate of iron, changing it to an inert coating which can be painted over.

(3) Stabilise the remaining rust.

Materials for these operations are in the Products Index under Rust solvents*. There are others also for dealing with the trouble, and the main thing to watch is that they are made by people of repute. Some cheaper compositions are on the market whose inadequacies are only discovered a year after they are applied.

After you have conscientiously dealt with the window in the manner described, rust may still reappear in time. That will no doubt be due to trouble breaking out in the rebate under the edge of the glass. We have said that rust spreads, and if it is present in adjacent parts it will eventually contaminate even the portions you have treated.

It would be too big a job to take out every pane throughout a house, derust the rebates and fit in new sheets of glass; so wait until the glass cracks, as no doubt it will. As we have already mentioned, rust is iron oxide and, in the oxidising process, expansion takes place to press against the edge of the glass and fracture it. Have you ever come downstairs in the morning and found an unaccountable crack in the pane of a steel sashed window? Don't blame your boy for his footballing activities before you examine the fault to see if rust in the rebate is not the culprit.

Peeling Paint

Windows are usually the first part of a house to disintegrate. They require repainting twice as often as do other surfaces for the following reasons.

Rain runs down the glass outside, enters a fractured paint-film or disintegrating putty rebate, wetting a wooden sash and rusting a metal one. Condensation does the same thing inside. The very thin putty here may crack on an upper window sash through its bottom rail being too weak to stand the strain, without bending, of repeated opening and closing. If you have such a window, it is a good idea to fit handles (Fig. 16C) to encourage the family to use the sides of the sash instead of the middle.

Rain can also run under the bottom rail of a casement window that is kept closed for a long period, collect there and work its way up by capillary attraction into the wood. That is one reason for a bottom rail rotting early, and why you should always paint its under edge. Inside, condensation runs down onto the bottom rail, between rail and stop, and underneath, causing the same trouble (Fig. 17A).

If the woodwork of a sash is sound, apart from the bottom rail which shows signs of rot, this rail can sometimes be replaced as is shown in Fig. 17B. Cut a new rail to size and with tenons to fit the existing mortises of the stiles. Saw it through at an angle. Secure each half in the corresponding mortise and join the cut parts together with brass screws which will not rust, counter-sinking the heads and filling in depressions with hard stopping*.

Another entry for moisture in a wooden sash is through

cracks forming at mortise and tenon joins which tend to 'give' when a window is used a lot. Fill these with hard stopping before painting.

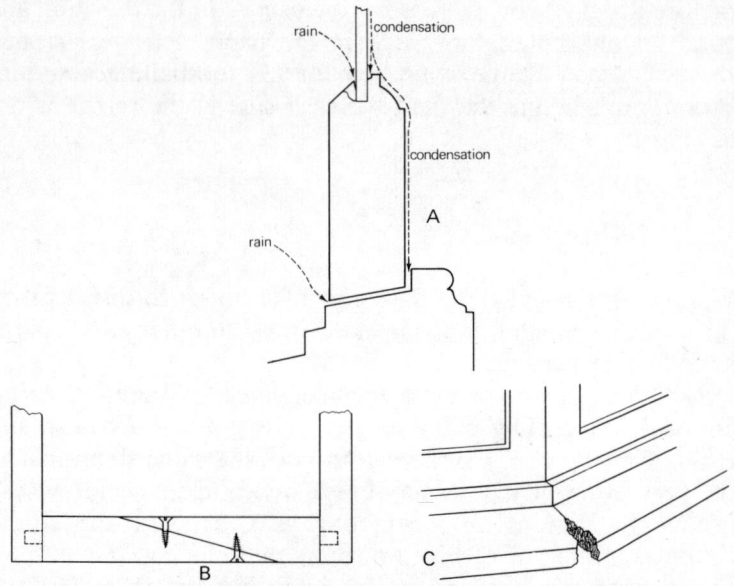

Fig. 17. Moisture damage to sashes and sills. A – Bottom of window sash affected by rain outside and condensation inside house. B – Replaced bottom rail. C – Rotted bay window sill

Frames

Paint may peel from window frames and the wood from which it is made start to rot. The cause of this is moisture seeping through from the surrounding masonry which may need repointing, or from damaged lutings, or from filled-in sill drip channels. This is dealt with in Chapter 10. If your frames are badly rotted the only thing to do is take them out and fit new ones. You can, however, often lengthen the life of wood that is not too far gone by boring a series of holes at intervals, pouring in clear wood preservative* and sealing over the holes with hard stopping. The principle behind this is that the preservative will work along with the grain of the wood and prevent the rot spreading any farther. Don't use coloured preservative or 'bleeding' will result.

New frames are always shop-primed before being built into brickwork with the idea of preventing entry of moisture. It would be better if they were given an undercoat and one finishing coat of paint as well. Better still if they were coated with aluminium primer sealer whose minute leafy texture provides a seal, like overlapping slates on the roof of a house.

Sills

Brick, stone and concrete window sills seldom give trouble but wooden ones do, especially if they are of oak or other highly porous woods.

Oak may not readily rot, but what happens is that paint applied on it 'bridges' over the pores, entrapping minute columns of air which expand under a hot sun, forming pimples. These burst and rain enters the pinholes thus formed. The remedy is to remove existing paint and apply a generous coat of wood primer diluted with about 15 per cent white spirit, brushing it on with a scrubbing motion so that it soaks in and lines the walls of the pores. When dry, apply another coat of primer, this time unthinned, and then follow with an undercoat and two finishing coats of an alkyd resin paint*.

Another reason for paint failure on oak is that the sill has not a sufficient slope. Oak has a ridgy texture, allowing small pools of rain to accumulate, and these weaken the paint film. Taking out a sill and re-aligning would be a big job; but you can scrape the surface to lower the ridges before painting, using a Skarsten scraper*.

A continuous window sill running round a bay window often becomes rotten at the joints (Fig. 17C). Cut out the rotted portions and, if the gap left is not too large, you can fill it with any form of hard or plastic stopping* reinforced, if necessary, with fibreglass. Where there is an extensive gap, you will have to make a clean cut to insert a new piece of wood, holding it in position with brackets screwed from underneath.

Leaded Windows

To remove a broken light for replacement in a leaded window, make diagonal cuts in the joints of the cames (strips of metal surrounding the light) with a sharp knife and prise up one flange of the groove holding the glass. Clean out the exposed rebate, fill with putty coloured with lamp-black to match the other joints and put in a new sheet of glass slightly less in size all round. If the pane follows an irregular shape, cut a thin cardboard template to hand to the glass merchant as a guide.

Press the flange back with a small piece of wood, paying special attention to the edges. Then fill the cuts in the cames with plastic metal stopping* or solder and, when hard, file smooth.

Discoloured cames can be freshened up quickly by brushing liquid blacklead – the stuff used on old-fashioned fire-grates – over the whole window, glass as well as cames. Leave to dry and brush with a stiff brush. The polish will flake off the glass, leaving it clean, but will adhere to the lead.

8
Bathrooms and Kitchens

Damage from Steam

Steam is the culprit that plays havoc with the decorations of bathrooms and kitchens.

In a bathroom it is bad enough – though bathing is spasmodic, allowing time for wall and ceiling areas to dry out. In a kitchen it is worse because vapour from cooking and washing is more or less continuous. Then again, the resistance of a kitchen is lowered because it is used, as often as not, quite carelessly.

If you do not want to redecorate these rooms every two or three years, greater attention than is customary should be paid to what is put on in the first place.

Distempers, water paints and ordinary wallpapers are OUT straight away. Lasting materials are needed and more care has to be taken over examination of what was previously applied than is the case with other rooms. For instance, if you brush a porous emulsion over a relatively impermeable, previously applied oil paint, steam will penetrate the former, condense against the latter and, as the entrapped water cannot regain the surface quickly enough to evaporate, it will collect behind and eventually push the emulsion off. This distressing business of condensation will be dealt with more thoroughly in Chapter 10.

Ceramic tiles are not always the complete answer. They certainly last a long time and are easily cleaned but, presenting a cold, hard, glossy surface as they do, they attract condensation to the extent that, if a bathroom ceiling were covered with them, annoying drops of moisture would fall on your head every time you took a bath. For this reason they are best kept for the lower reaches of a wall – particularly round bath, washbasin, sink and cooking stove – where dirt is more likely to find a harbour if it cannot be readily washed off.

For the upper parts of a wall, and for the ceiling of a room large enough for most of the condensation to disperse, an alkyd resin gloss paint* is as good as anything because it is easy to clean. But if water runs down every time you boil a kettle to leave an unsightly streak, change to an eggshell which is not so prone to drips but which will not last quite so long. A completely matt oil paint does not stand up to alternate wetting and drying at all well and should not be used where steam is about.

An alternative to an oil paint is an outdoor grade of emulsion paint* or a vinyl wall covering* – not an ordinary wallpaper. The former is fairly absorptive whereas the latter is easier to clean. For the reason given above, apply an emulsion to bare plaster or over an old emulsion – not over an old oil paint. With vinyl, use the mould-resisting adhesive recommended by the manufacturer.

When condensation is severe in a small room, you can use an anti-condensation paint* on the upper parts of a wall and also on the ceiling, or you can hang a polystyrene sheeting and decorate over that. The snag of this material is that, being soft, it is easily dented in a kitchen which is subject to more than customary wear and tear. Tiles made of polystyrene are easy to fix on a ceiling. Make sure they are of the flame-retardant type for the kitchen. Never place them over a cooking stove, and note the fire warning on page 33.

The part of a ceiling that comes over a bath is difficult to reach when sticking on tiles or subsequent cleaning. Make a temporary 'scaffolding' from a short plank of wood with a lip at each end to engage with the sides of the bath and prevent slipping (Fig. 18A). Protect the edge of the bath with cloth or paper.

You will see in Chapter 10 that if the walls and ceiling of a bathroom are kept warm there will be little likelihood of condensation forming. Where there is central heating you can have a radiator fixed. Direct electricity will be expensive and should

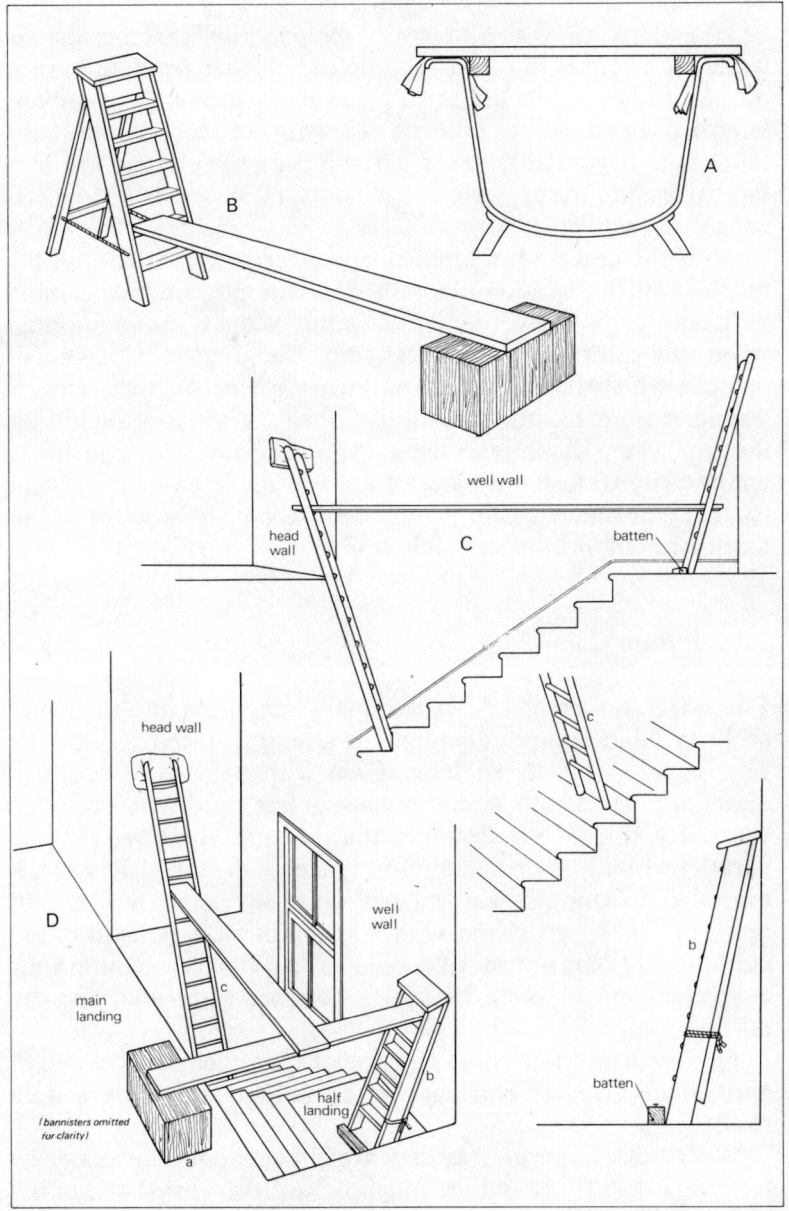

Fig. 18. Improvised scaffolding. A – To reach bathroom ceiling.
B – To reach living-room ceiling. C – To reach ceiling of a
straight stair. D – To reach ceiling of a turned stair

be considered only as a means of temporarily warming the air while the room is in use. If you do use electric heating, have it properly installed in the form of a tubular heater or a radiant lamp fixed sufficiently high on the wall not to be within easy reach (see page 100). Never carry a portable electric fire into the bathroom. Many serious accidents, even deaths, have been caused in that way.

As is the case with a kitchen, an extractor fan fitted into the outside wall or a window of a bathroom will reduce condensation.

Steam forms more quickly when hot water is in motion than when it is stationary. This means that the greatest damage will be done when running a bath and when letting the water out. If you have no extractor fan, always open the window slightly at the top when water is moving. Another thing you can do is temporarily to fasten a piece of hose to the hot water tap with its free end immersed in a little cold water already drawn, so that there will not be so much motion.

Bath Care

The glaze on a bath is powdered glass integrated into the metal shell, through a clay undercoat, at a temperature of 1,000°C. That is why it lasts so long. Even with the use of abrasive cleaners, a good bath should remain in fair condition for fifteen years. By employing cleansers that are not abrasive, such as paraffin, it will last considerably longer − particularly when a thorough cleaning is carried out only, say, once a week. In between times, rub round with a soapy or detergent-saturated cloth. If this does not shift the film, use a nylon pot scourer (not a scratchy metal one). Special nylon pads are sold for the purpose.

Never leave water standing in a bath for a lengthy period, in hard-water districts particularly, or pitting of the glaze may result.

When stains appear − as they are almost bound to sooner or later, particularly round the plughole and also at that end of the bath if taps are left dripping − use a bath stain remover*. Never use lavatory cleanser on a bath or you will take off the enamel.

When a bath gets to the stage when no amount of treatment

will restore it, the obvious remedy is to replace it with a new one. While you are about it, it is worth spending a few pounds more and investing in a really good bath*. It will repay you in the end.

You can, however, get a bath re-enamelled *in situ** at considerably less than the cost of a new one.

Painting a bath yourself is an arduous job and you have to bear in mind that no hand-applied paint can possibly have the wearing properties of the original finish that has been fused into the metal. To keep it in good order you should always turn the cold tap on first, allowing the water to warm gradually and give the different coefficients of expansion between paint and metal a chance to catch up with each other; and you will never be able to use bath salts or an abrasive cleanser.

Choose a bath enamel of repute* and follow the manufacturer's directions implicitly, particularly regarding preparatory cleaning and etching of the surface. Don't use the bath for a week after painting, to allow the film to harden.

Where one side of the bath adjoins a wall, lay a non-fluffy cloth or piece of paper over the near edge, so that skin grease from your arm does not contaminate it while you are attending to the far side. Start painting at the middle of the top edge of the far side, extending your laps of paint each way (alternately, to prevent a hard edge from forming) and downwards until that side is completed. Carry on around the ends and bottom and complete the near side and near edge last.

Tile Care

The cement joins between tiles on a bathroom wall often become dingy while the rest of the tiles are quite good.

Scrape out the surface grouting with a sharp-pointed knife. Mix waterproof grouting cement to a creamy consistency and rub it into the joints. Remove surplus with a sponge or cloth and, when dry, polish with a soft cloth.

If the surface of the tiles has become crazed stick new ceramic tiles* on top. A cheaper and quicker way is to apply two thin finishing coats of an alkyd resin paint*, diluting the first coat with a small quantity of white spirit. Don't use primer which is too oily, or undercoat which is too highly pigmented to adhere well.

A rule of painting is that nothing foreign must be allowed to come between paintfilm and substrate. This is even more important when painting tiles than the general run of surfaces because they are so hard that they cannot absorb any of the paint. It means that great care must be taken over preparatory cleaning to make sure that not the slightest trace of grease or dirt is left behind. And when you have finished cleaning, remove all signs of detergent with clear water. As this water may seep into the grouting, leave the surface for a day to dry thoroughly before applying the paint. Then leave the newly applied coating for a week to start oxidising before allowing too much steam to collect in the room.

If you have a tiled shelf at the end of the bath on which cosmetics and cleaning materials will be stood, a self-adhesive vinyl sheeting* will be even better than paint, because it has greater chemical resistance.

Basins and Water Closets

If the outsides of an earthenware w.c. pan and washbasin are getting dingy, you can freshen them up with bath enamel or with two finishing coats of an alkyd resin paint in the same way as you deal with tiles.

The insides, however, cannot be painted. The U-pipe of the w.c. pan is continuously immersed in water contaminated with acids from urine and excrement. The washbasin is used at least three times as frequently as is a bath and the alkali content of water it holds for washing (coming from soap) is bound to be more concentrated.

Even with daily use of a lavatory brush, the glaze of the inside of a w.c. pan will in time become worn and turn yellow. When a sprinkle of lavatory cleanser or bleach fails to keep it reasonably clean-looking, all you can do is to bail as much water as you can out of the U-pipe with a small vessel and mop up the remainder with an absorbent cloth. Then use an abrasive cleanser.

Condensation does not, as a rule, form on the underneath

portions of a kitchen sink because the sink is kept warm by hot water being used in it. The same applies to a bathroom wash-basin. But a w.c. cistern is always cold. Drips of water from underneath may fall on the floor, resulting in an annoying puddle or, if it is a high cistern, in embarrassing drips on your head. These can be reduced by sticking a piece of polystyrene sheeting on the under surface.

Kitchen and Bathroom Furniture

Scrape rusted parts of a worn refrigerator and rub with fine waterproof abrasive paper wetted with white spirit. Carry the rubbing operation onto the sound paint to reduce the gloss. Touch in the bad portions of metal with a rust remover*. Then paint the entire refrigerator with a polyurethane paint*, follow-ing the manufacturer's directions.

As polyurethane paint resists chemical attack better than does alkyd resin paint, use it on bathroom and kitchen cabinets and on kitchen chairs. The top of a wooden kitchen table can be covered with laminated plastic sheeting*.

Cut the sheeting *very slightly* oversize with a tenon saw held a little obliquely — that is, a few degrees off horizontal. This will give greater control over the saw and a smoother cut, and will prevent the stiff back of the saw from fouling the sheet.

The contact adhesive recommended by the manufacturer of the sheeting will stick firmly immediately the two surfaces are brought together; which means that you will not be able to shift the sheeting about to get it right without some form of a guide. Stick drawing pins temporarily into two adjoining edges of the table with the heads slightly protruding above the top and the sheet will fall into position first time. After the adhesive has hardened, file and glasspaper the edges to fit exactly.

Fitting a Canopy

A canopy and the pipe joining it to the outside wall, which one often sees in a factory, look ugly in a small kitchen. If you want a canopy, fix it not too far above the stove but at a distance to allow the housewife to peer under it into the cooking pans. The outlet duct can be of asbestos. Take a few bricks out of the wall with a cold chisel and hammer, to allow the pipe to pass through, and build round it afterwards with half and quarter bricks, using a mortar to match in with the remainder of the wall. See that the outlet does not directly face prevailing winds or the steam will be blown back in again. You may have to make a bend in the pipe and, if this is necessary, an extractor fan will have to be fitted at the mouth of the duct.

Fitting an Extractor Fan

An extractor fan is less of an eyesore than is a canopy. It can be fixed into a wall or into a window, whichever is the more convenient, bearing in mind the position of the source of steam and of the door leading into the kitchen from another room. It should be as high up as possible because steam and hot air rise.

A wall fan is fixed in a way similar to that of an outlet pipe of a canopy.

If you intend fixing it into a window, remove the sash and clean the glass thoroughly. Support the pane on a pad of felt or several sheets of newspaper. Determine the radius of the circle required to take the fan.

Make a trammel out of a piece of wood with a sharp-pointed nail driven through at one end and a hole to take the glass-cutter at the other, so that the distance between nail and cutter is equal to the radius you wish to cut. Grind a depression into the pane, indicating the centre of the extractor fan. Place the nail end of the trammel in this and cut the circle with the other end (Fig. 19) at (a). Do not allow the cutter to leave the surface until you have completed the circle.

Turn the pane over and 'run' it by pressing gently but firmly with a cloth pad. Turn the glass over again to its original position. Cut another circle (b) of radius about 20 mm. ($\frac{3}{4}$ in.) less than that of (a). This can be done freehand; it need not be perfect. Stand the glass upright with the cut away from you. Run (a) sharply all round with the handle of the cutter, then again run (b) in the same way.

Return the pane to its original position, cuts uppermost, and make diagonal cuts (c).

Stand the pane upright with cuts away from you and starting from the centre, 'run' cuts (c) segment by segment. Each segment should now fall out.

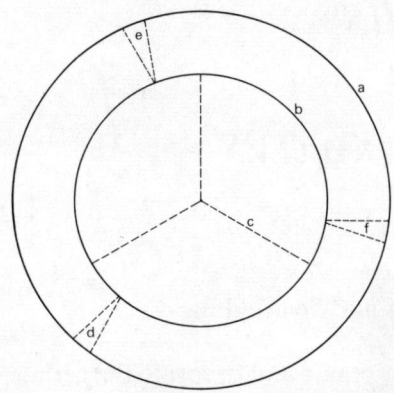

Fig. 19. Cutting glass for an extractor fan

Make a V-cut at (d) and tap out. Make two cuts at (e) and (f). 'Run' gently and the whole of the remainder of the centre will fall out — we hope! If it does not, get a glass merchant to do the job for you.

9
Halls and Stairways

Ladders and Scaffolding

You can repair and decorate the ceiling of a room from household steps, or, if you don't wish to keep running up and down and moving the steps, by arranging a make-do scaffolding consisting of a plank joining a convenient rung to an upturned box, as is shown in Fig. 18B. But this won't do for the ceiling of a stairwell.

There are patented adaptable metal ladders which fold one way to enable them to be used on stairs, and the other way for reaching other awkward heights. Or you can improvise your own with parts of an extension ladder, planks and household steps.

To reach the ceiling and top of the walls of a straight stairway, for instance, stand a ladder on a convenient stair tread with its foot against the riser and lean it against the head wall. No doubt the head wall will be of lath and plaster, so spread the weight by tying a length of wood to the top so that each end rests over a stud (timber framework inside the wall).

Stand a shorter ladder on the landing, leaning against the opposite wall, and join a convenient round of each with a scaffold plank. The shorter ladder will have no protective stair riser to prevent it from slipping, so rough-nail a batten of wood to the landing in front of it (Fig. 18C). A 2·5-m. span would require a plank 50 mm. thick; in imperial measure, 2 in. thick for an 8 ft 6 in. span. Anything longer would have to be proportionately thicker.

A stairway with a right-angled corner can be scaffolded as is shown in Fig. 18D. An upturned box (a) stands on the landing at the top of the stairs. Household steps (b) are closed and kept from slipping by a batten nailed onto the half landing. These rest against the well wall. A part of an extension ladder (c) stands on the stairs and rests against the head wall.

Other designs of stair can be accommodated by adapting these simple devices. Indeed, there are few heights that cannot be reached if you think things well out in advance. If there is any danger of side-slipping with your scaffolding, lash everything firmly. A fall on a banister handrail or newel post could be serious.

You should always start at the window end when wallpapering a room. But with a stairwell, hang the first length on the well wall where it joins the head wall and then butt subsequent lengths on at each side, working in both directions.

Squeaking Stairs

Fig. 20 shows how typical domestic stairs are assembled. The design can, of course, vary slightly.

A riser is tongued into a tread and a block of wood is glued underneath the join – for extra strength and to prevent the join

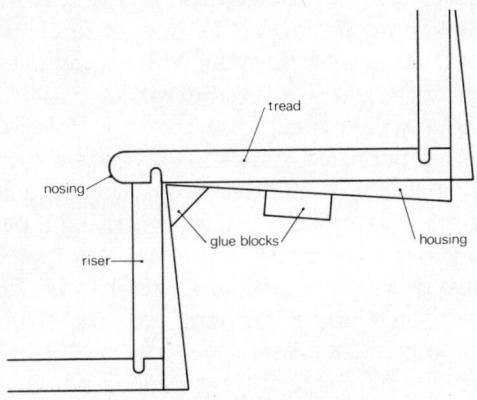

Fig. 20. Construction of stairs

from 'giving'. Both risers and treads are housed, wedged and nailed into the strings (side pieces).

If the glued block falls off or if any of the joins become loose, two planes of wood will rub together and cause squeaking every time anyone puts his foot on that tread.

The fault is easily corrected where the underneath part of a stairway is left exposed. But when it is lathed and plastered, or otherwise covered, the sheathing will have to be removed to enable you to effect a permanent cure. Fortunately, it is usually only one or two treads that squeak and you can often put them right by applying penetrating oil at the joints without removing anything underneath. This will have to be repeated every time you take up the carpet for cleaning. Be sparing with the oil or it will bleed through the carpet and stain it.

Try to discourage your family from stamping up the stairs, and there will be less likelihood of the joins becoming loosened. Damage is not caused by the weight of a person so much as by the way he (or she) places his or her foot on the treads. In mounting stairs most people put the ball of the foot near the front of the tread and slide it towards the riser. This 'scraping' should be avoided. Place the foot on each tread as though you were walking.

Carpeting Stairs

A good underlay is essential if a room carpet is to have a long life. It is even more important to have a thick pad tacked to each tread of a stairway before the stair carpet is laid. Not only will these preserve the life of the carpet, particularly at the nosing, but they will reduce noise.

Stair clips susperseded stair rods to keep a carpet firmly in position, and these in turn have given way to grippers which are wood or metal laths with spikes, following a pattern similar to those now used for fitted room carpets (page 26). These enable a brush or vacuum cleaner to get into the corners unimpeded, leaving only those corners between string, riser and tread to harbour dust. Here you can nail small triangular blocks of wood; or plastic fittings can be bought for the purpose: see Fig. 21A.

Whether you choose grippers made of wood or metal will be determined by the thickness of the carpet. Buy them at the same time and at the same shop as you buy the carpet, and the shopkeeper will advise you on this point. You can screw grippers through the pads to reduce the number of tacks used in securing the pads. Grippers are not really suitable for foam- or rubber-backed carpets and here you will have to resort to clips or rods.

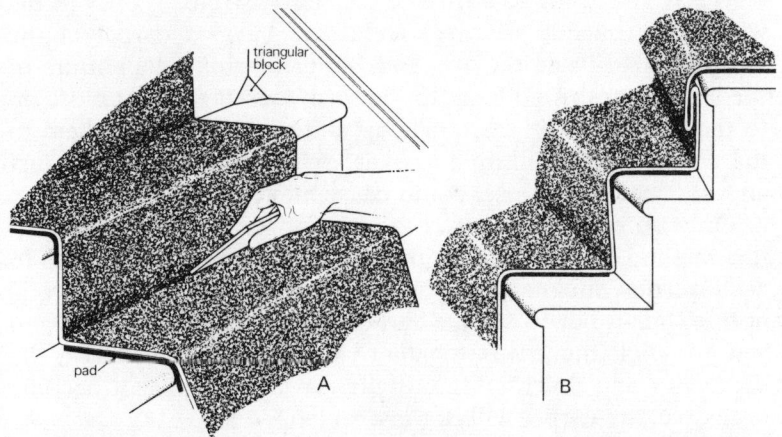

Fig. 21. Carpeting of stairs. A – Pressing carpet onto grippers. B – Carpet at turn with surplus at narrow part left free, to be folded underneath and tacked to risers

To measure the length of carpet required, place a piece of string across a tread, over the nosing and down the riser until it reaches the next tread. Multiply this length by the number of treads and add half a metre (1 ft. 6 in.) so that the carpet may be moved up or down once a year, during spring-cleaning time, to even out wear. If your stairs turn round in a quarter circle, take the outside measurement. Note: a pile carpet should be moved up or down. If you turn it, so that the top comes to the bottom, the pile will run in the wrong direction, and any scuffing of the feet on the treads will wear it unduly and tend to make the carpet ruck.

To lay a stair carpet, roughly chalk each tread showing the position of the carpet. If you are using wooden grippers, screw one into each tread and riser between these marks and about 10 mm. ($\frac{1}{2}$ in.) from the join between the tread and riser. Don't fix grippers at a turn of the stairs – here you will have to use tacks. Metal grippers are generally angled and must be secured right up to the join.

Starting at the top, tuck the carpet under the landing floor covering and tack down. Stretch tightly and bang the carpet into the join between tread and riser, over the spikes of each gripper, using a piece of plywood or hardboard (Fig. 21A).

When you come to a turn of the stairs, stretch tightly at the wide part (outside the arc) and leave surplus carpet at the narrow part (inside the arc) free. After reaching the bottom of the stairs you can go back to the turn, tack the carpet close up to the join, fold the free parts up and under and tack them to the risers. Don't fold up and over, or the fold will collect dust and, if it becomes loose, could cause an accident (Fig. 21B).

Only on rare occasions is the turn of stairway so sharp that this method is impossible without bunching up the free sides to a dangerous thickness. If your stairs are so designed, there is nothing for it but to cut the carpet at each riser of the turn and sew or stick the edges together. You cannot then move the carpet up and down and, as wear on each tread will become excessive, the carpet will not last so long.

To lift a stair carpet secured by grippers, start at the bottom, push into the join between tread and riser and pull up.

Stairs seen in some modern open-plan houses are built like a step-ladder and have no risers. Each tread has to be covered individually with cork or rubber stuck on.

Colour

Before leaving this chapter we would stress that colour schemes for halls and stairs should be bright and welcoming. As some halls are ridiculously small or narrow, use light, cool colours and the entrance to the house will appear larger.

10
Damp Walls and Ceilings

Causes of Damp

Damp, as opposed to flooding, is commonly reckoned as a fault that does not necessitate immediate action. If it is left unattended for too long, however, not only is it an eyesore, ruining decorations, but it can cause deterioration in plaster, dry rot in wood and rust in iron and steel. That is quite apart from danger to the health of the householder and his family.

If you can trace the cause of a damp patch straight away you will be lucky. All that remains to do is to put right whatever is wrong. But if, as is quite as likely, the patch appears unaccountable, you will be in a better position than a builder or surveyor to trace its cause; living on top of the trouble, you can observe it in various temperatures and in changing conditions of humidity. A professional man may devote only an hour or so at one time for examination, whereas you can give the fault occasional glances and intermittent thought over a period – which will take only a few minutes a day.

But you must know what to look for.

Damp may come from inside a house (condensation) or from outside (penetration of rain), from up above (roof), from down below (faulty damp-proof course) or from inside a wall (interstitial trouble).

Wherever condensation is the culprit, a whole room may be affected. Where one wall only is damp through condensation it will generally be an outside wall which naturally is colder than an inside one, and the damp will no doubt continue to its extremities. Sometimes, however, condensation can be in patches only.

As a rule, interstitial damp spreads to the whole of an outside wall.

Moisture from outside generally leaves isolated damp patches inside; only in very bad cases will it affect the whole wall.

Damp coming from the roof can discolour the ceiling or walls. In all cases, apart from flooding, it will be confined to patches.

Although moisture emanating from down below will dampen the whole of the floor, it may spread in patches only on the lower part of a wall. But if, as is often the case, a do-it-yourselfer applies a silicone waterproofing solution without thought to the outside and inside of the affected wall, his misguided labours can cause the entrapped damp, which cannot now reach the surface and evaporate, to rise by capillary attraction and come out in an upstairs room.

Following the procedure of a doctor diagnosing a physical ailment let us examine the most obvious causes of damp first, proceeding step by step to the more obscure, and giving remedies as we go.

Condensation

The air we breathe is slightly moist. If it were completely dry our health would suffer perhaps as much as it would if humidity were at 100 per cent.

A given volume of air can hold only a certain amount of water, after which it reaches saturation point and the surplus moisture is deposited on any surface that is fortuitously there. This often happens in a kitchen when cooking or washing is in progress; and the remedy is either to fix a canopy over the stove or sink with an outlet through the outside wall, or to increase ventilation by opening windows (a louvre window* is the most effective) or by fitting an extractor fan so that the steamy air is drawn outside to disperse. (The fitting of a canopy and fan has been dealt with in Chapter 8.)

Now suppose there is no excessive build-up of steam: condensation can occur through the atmosphere of a room becoming moist from the human body and breath – say, in an unventilated bedroom. This moisture may not be sufficient to condense on everything within the room because warm air will warm the furniture; but when the air comes into contact with the relatively cold surface of an outside wall or window it will itself become cold and so decrease in volume. As saturation point will now be reached at a lower temperature, the air will no longer be able to hold the water – which will be deposited on the wall.

When warm damp weather suddenly follows a cold spell, a building structure will not itself immediately warm up and moist air coming in through windows will condense on relatively cold walls, ceilings, floors and furniture. In a day or two this type of condensation will vanish – providing the building is of fairly heavy construction. Increased ventilation will be of no help here. The remedy is to increase the warmth of the room and its components, or to insulate the wall.

The first remedy might prove expensive unless central heating were being installed in any case. It is not sufficient to turn on heat half an hour before, say, taking a steamy bath. The walls must be allowed to warm up and that takes time, in some cases extending to days. A warning about electric stoves in bathrooms is given in Chapter 13. Paraffin stoves are not of much use because they actually give out moisture during combustion – roughly an amount the same as the volume of oil burned.

Walls may be insulated by battening and sheathing with plasterboard or insulation board. A simpler way is to line them with polystyrene sheeting (see fire warning on page 33), over which emulsion paint or wallpaper may be used; or to paint them with an anti-condensation paint *. The idea of mixing cork chippings in paint is not advisable because, although cork insulates, it will rely more upon its powers of absorption; and although water that is absorbed will not be apparent on the surface, it is still there and can damage the substrate.

Any amount of heat in a room will not warm up a window unless a radiator is placed immediately underneath, because of the cooling action of the air outside. If a radiator is not placed in that position, draught often results even if the window is kept closed, through the interchange of warm and cool air.

Fitting double glazing is effective because it entraps a column of air between two panes of glass and this acts as an insulator. But installing an extra pane of glass is expensive and it is done comparatively cheaply only when a house is being built. Many do-it-yourself double-glazing kits on the market are good; some are not adequate, and others encourage the growth of mould between the panes. For this reason, in our opinion, it is advisable to bring experts in to do the installation.

Sometimes condensation takes place in the most unlikely of rooms.

We recently encountered an instance in a bedroom on the first floor of a house. Dampness persisted in a wall in spite of experimentation with various remedies. Then we noted that the bedroom door, always left open, was immediately at the top of the stairs. At the bottom was the kitchen door, also always left open. Steam was passing through the door from the cooking stove and into the hall. Being lighter than the surrounding air it rose up the stairwell, entered the bedroom and deposited itself on the wall. This was proved by keeping both bedroom and kitchen doors closed over a period, after which condensation ceased.

Pattern Staining

Have you ever noticed a lath and plaster ceiling that has become dark with dirt, showing lightish-coloured broad lines running across a room? Follow the light-coloured lines and you will find they come immediately beneath wooden ceiling joists. Wood is a good insulator; and so that part of the ceiling immediately below remains warm while the intervening plaster becomes relatively cool. Moisture-charged air rises and is deposited on the cool parts in quantities so small that they may not be noticed, but sufficient to cause dust to stick — whereas this does not happen where the plaster comes over a warm joist. If this occurs in your house, you can either wash the ceiling frequently to remove the dirt or, to effect a permanent cure, lift up the floorboards in the room upstairs and insert quilted or granular insulating material* between the joists. 'Pattern staining' is the name given to this trouble!

If you add too much insulating material you could reverse the process, encouraging dirt to follow the outline of the joists with relatively clean stretches of ceiling in between. This is called 'reverse pattern staining'. It is often seen in factories where cold steel ceiling joists are used. In houses it may take the form of dark spots covering cold metal nail-heads which have been insufficiently punched in and filled over.

Painting and Condensation

What has been said about condensation within a house also takes place outside for similar reasons. Sudden changes of temperature altering the saturation point of the air cause dew to form on the grass and housetops early in the morning and late in the afternoon – and on doors, window frames, sills and masonry surfaces. Though it may not be in sufficient quantities to be apparent it will affect the adhesion of paint; and that is why it is dangerous to start painting exteriors in the morning until the sun has evaporated moisture and warmed the air, and also why evening painting outside is not advisable.

As the most critical period in the life of a paint film is a week after it has been applied, don't allow too much steam to accumulate in a room during that period.

In Chapter 8 we dealt with the dangers of applying porous emulsion paint over a previously gloss-painted wall. A small area of damp on an emulsion-painted kitchen wall once puzzled us until we removed the emulsion. Underneath we found that a painter had wiped out his brush, used with oil paint, on this part of the wall, leaving a dense, relatively cold patch on which moisture had condensed.

Rain Penetration

Rain can penetrate a brick wall if the mortar joins between the bricks have deteriorated. The only remedy here is to patch up bad places or repoint completely (see Chapter 2). Cracked cement rendering may not always result in damp in the corresponding part of the inside wall. Rain *could* run between rendering and wall and enter at a place lower down.

Where pointing is sound, the bricks may have become porous with age, causing damp to enter — particularly if the wall is in an exposed position. After examining the possibilities of other factors being responsible for entry of moisture, you may come to the conclusion that this is the trouble. If so, clean down the outside and give it two applications of a silicone waterproofing solution — a treatment that will last ten years; and two fresh applications at the end of that period can easily be brushed on. Silicone solutions do not interfere with the existing colour of a wall. Some of them may be tinted to obviate the risk of 'misses' in your brushwork, and the colour additive soon fades.

Apart from keeping out rain, silicones prevent the wall from becoming excessively cold because water always cools a surface on evaporation. This treatment will not function, however, if the pointing has gone or if a rendering has cracked. Decayed mortar and cracks must be seen to first.

Even when new, bricks used in house construction are porous. Immerse one in a bucket of water and you can confirm this. But rain seldom beats against a wall for a sufficiently long period for it to do much damage. An overflowing gutter or leaky downpipe, however, can cause extreme saturation. Check pipes and gutters in the vicinity of the wet patch. Check also the angle of any protruding overflow pipes leading from water tanks and cisterns. Go inside, depress the ballcock with your hand and note how the water flows out. If it runs under the pipe back onto the wall, bend the pipe down at a more acute angle. Poke out cobwebs and congealed paint that may have accumulated inside the pipe.

When an extremely solid engineering type of brick has been used — and this is seldom — porosity is naturally lessened. But mortar tends to shrink on drying; and, in doing so, may cause the jointing to become detached here and there from the bricks it bonds together, leaving microscopic cracks through which rain will penetrate by capillary attraction. Providing the cracks are not easily seen by the naked eye, a silicone waterproofing solution applied outside should cure the trouble.

Dampness often occurs under a window. This may be due to faulty joins between the bricks or to porous bricks in the surrounding part of the wall; in which case, patch up the pointing (Chapter 2) and apply silicone waterproofing outside locally. Perhaps the lutings have cracked (mortar fillets between window frame and adjoining masonry — see Fig. 22A), allowing rain to enter. Cracking of lutings is caused through

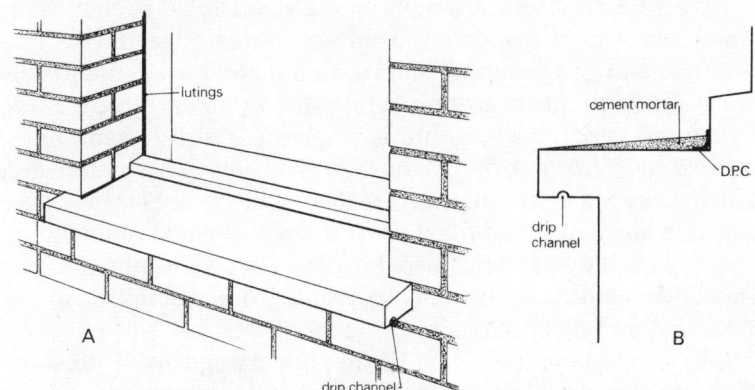

Fig. 22. A — Window showing lutings and drip channel. B — Rectifying a badly sloped sill

shrinkage, subsidence or heavy traffic outside shaking the structure. Rake out the joins and refill them with mastic compound* obtainable at your paintshop. This material never properly hardens and 'gives' with structural movement.

You may wonder why mastic is not used for glazing windows. It can be, and you can paint over it, but it is not entirely satisfactory for this purpose because it tends to wrinkle on forming a surface skin.

To digress, if you can discourage your family from banging doors — all of them, particularly the front door — lutings and all pointing will last considerably longer. Slamming and banging is quite unnecessary and jars the whole structure of a house, causing it to shudder.

A window sill may not be tilted forward sufficiently so that, instead of throwing rain clear, it allows water to run back into the wall. A wooden one can be replaced at the correct angle.

The surface of a stone or concrete sill can be roughened with a cold chisel and hammer and a layer of three parts by volume of sand and one of cement mortar, with a bonding agent added*, floated on top at the correct angle. If the wooden window frame touches the existing sill you will have to insert a vertical damp-proof course – a narrow strip of bituminous felt will do – otherwise moisture may seep into the wood from the new fillet by capillary attraction and rot it (Fig. 22B).

As a rule, tiled sills are built in at a steep angle so that water falling on top drips down from the outer edge. Stone and concrete sills are generally sloped on top and horizontal underneath. This could mean that rain will run down the edge and follow the under surface until it reaches the wall to saturate it, were it not for a drip channel – a groove cut underneath causing the water to fall clear of the wall (Fig. 22). Make sure that this channel is not filled up with cobwebs and old paint.

Drip channels should also be cut in wooden sills and the underside painted to prevent moisture from seeping in to rot the wood and push the paint off the topside.

Climbing plants are often blamed for dampness. With some creepers this is unfair – virginia creeper, for instance, whose foliage falls down at such a steep angle that it actually sheds rain. The greatest danger comes from plants, such as ivy, that cling to walls by suckers which fasten onto the mortar, disintegrating it. An additional disadvantage of such clinging plants is that domiciled insects will enter your bedroom through an open window – but that hardly comes within the scope of the subject of damp patches.

The Roof

If you have a cracked roofing tile you may think that rain entering will cause a wet patch on the ceiling immediately below (Fig. 23 at (a)). So it will, if a lot of water enters unhindered. But if there is only a drip and a rafter lies immediately underneath, the water could run down the rafter until it reaches an obstruction (Fig. 23 at (b)) and drip there. If there is no obstruction, it will flow down to penetrate the wall, causing a slight stain at the corner of a bedroom ceiling (Fig. 23 at (c)).

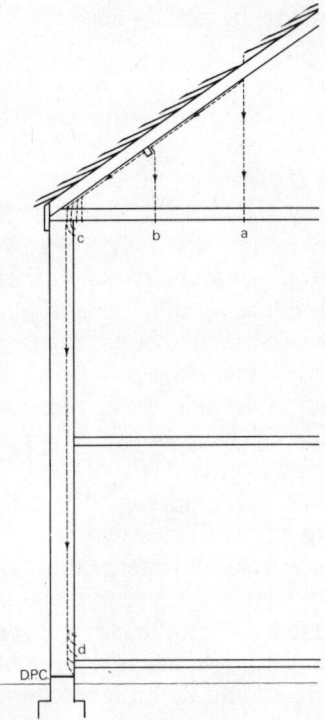

Fig. 23. A misplaced or broken roofing tile can cause damp patches in several places.

When the drip is very slight it could penetrate the brickwork and run down inside the wall until it reaches the damp-proof course where it will accumulate to make a massive stain close to the floor (Fig. 23) at (d).

Mending a roof is dealt with in Chapter 1.

Faulty Damp-proof Course

Bricks are porous. We repeat this because it has a direct bearing on what follows. When a wall is built directly on top of damp subsoil, moisture will seep up by capillary attraction, rot the skirting board and form a damp patch immediately above. But where a damp-proof course (a layer of slate, asphalt, copper, bituminous felt or other impermeable material) is let into a horizontal join between the bricks near the ground and below the flooring, this process is arrested.

In modern houses the d.p.c. is at least two bricks up from ground level so that subsoil moisture wets only those bricks below the course. You can easily trace the position of your d.p.c. by scratching the surface of mortar jointing that is near ground level and looks a little wider than the remainder. In houses built fifty years ago the course was let in immediately above surrounding soil; with such a d.p.c. there is great danger of moss and rubbish piling up outside and giving a free passage for damp to by-pass it. Similar trouble can be caused by having a flower bed with soil heaped against the upper courses of bricks. The first thing to do, therefore, in checking a d.p.c., is to go round the outside of your house and make sure that the bottom part of the wall is clear.

Houses built in the early part of the last century will not have a d.p.c. In those days reliance was placed upon a specially solid brick to stop the rise of water. Old houses built of hard stone such as granite also may not have them, though the snag here is that the mortar bonding the stones together may allow a passage for damp. When large, heavy blocks of an impermeable stone were used, walls would be built on the dry-wall principle – one on top of the other and pointing added afterwards outside. As long as the pointing remains sound, such walls will not become damp by rising moisture.

Damp-proof courses should last for the life of a house but they may become broken in places by subsidence or by war damage. Sometimes a weak d.p.c. will allow an upsurge of water from a downpipe that has cracked below the surface of the soil. The damaged pipe should be uncovered and the cracked portion replaced, otherwise in time a dangerous underground pool will form. If localised damage to a d.p.c. results in a small damp patch, knock out a few bricks with a hammer and cold chisel and replace the damaged course with new, allowing a generous overlap. The bricks can then be replaced.

Where damp is extensive, showing that most of a d.p.c. has deteriorated, the best thing to do is to call in specialists who may employ an electro-osmotic process * which does not interfere with the structure of a wall. This breaks capillary attraction by playing the odds between positive and negative charges in water.

Damp under a solid concrete floor is due to breakages in or absence of a sub-floor d.p.c. Break up the concrete with a heavy hammer and pickaxe and remove the debris. Lay a moisture barrier such as heavy duty polythene sheeting over a thin mortar (one part cement and three of sand) screed, generously overlapping joins, then screed over with more mortar 50 mm. (2 in.) thick, and continue the sheeting up the sides of the walls all round the room to the top of the screed. It is better not to lay linoleum or other impervious covering over such a floor. Rush or plastic matting is porous and will allow the floor to breathe.

Cavity Walls

Don't think that cavity wall construction is a certain cure for damp. The outside layer of bricks can become saturated, supercharging the entrapped air between the outer and inner sheathing and, during a sudden change of temperature, wetting the inner sheathing. If the inner sheathing is porous or thin, moisture will exude through to the inside of the house. The remedy here is to have an insulating membrane inserted in the cavity *.

Here is a simple example of what can happen within a cavity – in this case, a wooden garden shed.

The interior had been sheathed with medium hardboard and decorated with emulsion paint, leaving an insulating column of air to keep out extremes of heat and cold. Warm moist air entered the cavity from outside. So long as the shed was occupied and the heater kept on, the saturated moisture worked its way outside again and evaporated. But when a change in temperature occurred during the night, condensation leached through and this caused a discoloration of the emulsion.

A more serious cause of damp patches in cavity brick walls is where loose mortar has fallen on the metal ties which hold the two walls together, forming a bridge over which moisture passes from the outer to the inner sheathing. A careless bricklayer can also drop mortar into the cavity in the process of building until it reaches a dangerous height, turning the bottom part of the wall solid – and highly porous at that!

This is just plain faulty workmanship, and the only thing you can do, apart from pulling down the house and rebuilding, is to line the wall inside with metal-backed lining paper or seal in an isolated stain with aluminium primer sealer.

Interstitial Damage

Interstitial condensation can take place in a solid wall when the air outside is cold and well below saturation point and inside is warm and moist. About two-thirds of the inside of the bricks will become impregnated with warm, damp air which will condense *inside* the wall where it meets the cold air. This moisture could soak back inside if the sun is not strong enough to cause it to evaporate, or if the outside of the wall is coated with an impermeable paint (Fig. 24). Paint will keep out a deluge of rain, but a moisture-laden atmosphere will penetrate it.

The reverse could happen. On a warm, damp day, saturated air will penetrate the bricks from outside, meeting cold air coming from an unheated room.

Internal damp caused in this way will be only occasional and can be put right by sticking metal-backed or bitumen-coated paper over the affected wall to form a vapour barrier and seal in the resulting stain. It can be avoided by increasing the ventilation of the room.

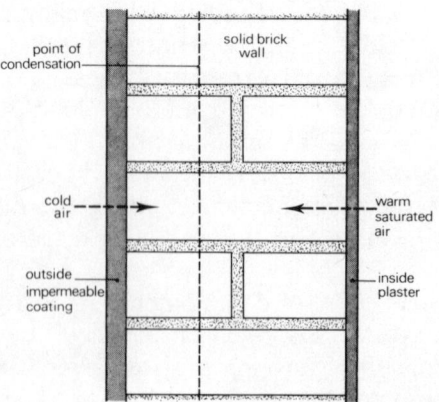

Fig. 24. Interstitial condensation

11
Rot
in
Timber

Dry rot, and its meeker cousin known by the misleading name of wet rot, are part of nature's means of getting rid of old dead wood and turning it into humus to fertilise soil in readiness for new growth. But if a householder allowed nature to have its own way, his home would soon be in ruins. Fortunately a new house built on scientific principles and kept in a good state of repair is not so likely to develop rot as is an old house erected by men who acted more by hunch than by knowledge.

Why dry rot? And why wet rot?

Dry rot is caused through the activity of a weeping fungus, one that carries its own water as it gropes its way around timber by means of thick threads, known as hyphae, which combine to form a white 'wool' or thin silvery sheets tinged with lilac patches, known as mycelium. The fruit body is like a pancake with a corrugated centre, and fungus spores (the equivalent of seeds) are so light in weight that they are readily carried in the air in countless millions. Wood that is affected by the dry-rot fungus becomes dark in colour and breaks into large cubes. Instead of the fresh resinous odour associated with sound wood there is a fusty, mushroomy smell.

The danger of this species of fungus is that it can start germinating in damp wood and spread through brickwork, plaster and even over steel girders, carrying moisture with it, to affect dry, sound timber at a distance as far away as 3 metres (10 ft).

Wet rot, more accurately described as cellar fungus (other species are not frequently encountered in Britain), requires wood that remains wet for a period to enable the spores to germinate. As it does not carry its own supply of water, once the source of moisture has been stopped it becomes moribund; that is to say, it apparently dies but can come back to life and break out again if circumstances suit it – but not unless. The threads by which it spreads form a pattern like blood vessels and are not nearly so thick as those of the dry-rot fungus. They are light brown to start with, turning to dark brown or black. There may be no obvious fruiting body; if there is, it is in the form of an olive-brown pancake.

Dry rot can quickly cause the complete destruction of timber in a building. And even when new timber replaces diseased it can infect the new unless a chemical fungicide is applied which is poisonous to it. Wet rot, though occurring twice as frequently as dry rot, is not nearly so destructive – though it must be attended to. It can work under a paintfilm so that the only symptom that shows on the surface is a waviness. If you see such signs, say, on a skirting board, plunge in a sharp-pointed knife. If the blade sinks easily, rip out the board and investigate further.

There is another form of rot which is not really rot because incipient decay (a breaking down of the wood structure through exposure to weather) is responsible rather than a fungus. This often shows on wooden window sills that are left unpainted. The surface of the timber becomes defibrated and furry. Once it is scraped no further trouble is likely and it can be repainted.

From this brief description of the fungi causing wood to rot (but not incipient decay) you will see that the steps taken to overcome the trouble must be drastic.

All infected timber and apparently sound wood for at least one metre beyond the farthest sign of decay must be cut away and burned. Sawdust from the cutting operation and chippings must be swept up and also burned. New timber must be treated with a fungicidal fluid * to prevent reinfestation. Sound existing timber must also be treated after thorough cleaning of the area with a wirebrush. Adjacent walls should be wirebrushed and soaked with the fungicide, after powdery droppings have been swept up.

As damp and a still atmosphere comprise the nursery of the trouble it is of no use taking protective measures unless you also trace the source of the damp and eradicate it by one of the means shown in Chapter 10. Air bricks should be cleaned out and more inserted, if necessary, at a distance of $1\frac{1}{4}$ m. (4 ft) from one another. They should be facing on each side of the house, not staggered, to ensure a through current of air un-obstructed by solid sleeper walls. A good way of ensuring adequate underfloor ventilation is by the installation of a fire-place relying upon underfloor draught* for efficient combustion.

Many years ago we moved into a house thirty years old which had been passed as 'sound' by a surveyor.

In taking up floorboards on the ground floor in readiness for electrical rewiring we were assailed by a pungent mushroomy odour and, with the aid of a torch, saw large clusters of beauti-fully coloured 'mushrooms' clinging to joists and sleeper walls. Not much was known about the dry-rot fungus in those days, and so we got a builder to scrape off the growths and lay new boards. Within six months the leg of a kitchen chair went through the floor and, on inspection, new growths were seen.

We applied to the Forest Products Research Laboratory for help and were advised to replace the flooring once again with new, and treat everything with a solution of sodium fluoride*. Sufficient crystals were ordered to make 90 gallons of solution and, after all the mess had been cleared up, new wood, old sound wood, sleeper walls and concrete base were given two generous applications.

Some of the wall plates could not be moved without under-pinning. Fortunately they were not too far gone, so we bored holes at 18-in. intervals, mixed up sodium fluoride to a mustard consistency and squeezed it into each hole with a motor-car grease gun, the idea being that if ever the wood became damp again, moisture would dissolve the paste which would be sucked into the grain, killing any fungus spores that happened to be there.

Rainwater gutters were checked, of course. Downpipes and gulleys were made sound and more air bricks inserted facing one another at each side of the house. New joists were fitted so that their end grain did not butt on to an outside wall without being covered with bituminous felt.

Removable trapdoors were fashioned by cutting three of the new floorboards in each room so that their ends came over adjoining joists, leaving just sufficient space for descent once a year to check that everything was all right. Everything is all right to this day!

Sodium fluoride is cheap but very poisonous and tends to leach out. Where damp is persistent it can cause efflorescence in infected plaster. Today's fungicides are based on penta-chlorophenol and sodium pentachlorophenate. When in spirit, these can result in staining, but that doesn't matter if the parts to be treated are below floor level. To be on the safe side, buy a proprietary fungicidal fluid* which contains an insecticide to protect against woodworm as well.

Small attacks of dry and wet rot, or attacks in their early stages, can be overcome by a householder prepared to undertake some pretty hard work on the lines indicated in this chapter. In the case of widespread infection, it is better to call in wood preservation experts*. The best of these will conduct a free survey and guarantee their treatment for twenty years. They should be members of the British Wood Preserving Association which lays down a code of practice.

It is also possible to insure your timbers against damage by rot.

12
Woodworm

The depredations caused by wood-boring beetles were at one time associated only with ancient buildings and old furniture; and a few woodworm holes here and there were looked upon as providing authentic antiquity. Indeed, manufacturers of reproduction pieces have been known to bore holes by hand to make their work look what it is not.

Some made a fair job of it; but their workmanship was not so perfect as the holes made by genuine woodworm. With the exception of weevil holes (page 92), these are perfectly circular or elliptical and so precise that their edges are devoid of even the slightest trace of furriness which results from the sharpest of man-made boring tools. There should therefore be no fear of your mistaking them for holes made by nails having been driven in and subsequently withdrawn.

A friend recently treated the door of a house into which he had moved with woodworm fluid, and then discovered that the holes in it were caused through the dart-playing activities of a previous owner. Obviously he did not know what he was supposed to be looking for.

Damage Done

It is really only during the last thirty years that woodworm has been taken seriously. We now know that it can completely ruin furniture and, if left to its own devices in the structural timbers of a house, can eventually cause collapse. We also know that three out of every five homes in Britain are affected, and one out of every five built since the last war.

At the turn of the century the knowledge builders had of stresses and strains was not what it is today and, to be on the safe side, they often used timbers much thicker than was necessary. Wood was cheap compared with what it is now and waste did not add substantially to the cost of building. Builders may not have realised it, but that thickness and width gave the 'extra' that allowed for the weakening effects of insect bore holes. Nowadays little or no tolerance is allowed.

But there is no cause for alarm. By the use of woodworm fluids* and the exercise of patience you can eradicate the pest from your home.

Types of Beetle

Of the many species of wood-boring insect the most common in Britain are given below.

With a few exceptions, it is the grub that does the boring, not the beetle; but the beetle has wings and most of them can flit from place to place, laying their eggs wherever they land.

Fortunately they are lazy creatures and prefer to walk a short distance rather than fly. That is why the holes of the common furniture beetle are generally in clusters and why the bottom rail of a door is often riddled. The beetle wanders over the floor until it reaches a door and lays its eggs on the rough, unpainted bottom edge. The grubs hatch out and work their way into the wood, feed on it and eventually emerge by the quickest route – through the painted surface of the bottom rail.

Common furniture beetle. This is the cause of 80 per cent of infestations. It is chocolate brown in colour and about 3 mm. ($\frac{1}{8}$ in.) long. The female lays between twenty and sixty eggs at a time in cracks and crevices of timber, and these hatch out into off-white coloured grubs which bore into the wood and feed on it as they tunnel backwards and forwards with the grain. After about three years they return near the surface where they pupate; and then, in the form of a new beetle, bite their way out and start breeding all over again. The entry holes are too small to be seen; but the exit holes, being 1 or 2 mm. ($\frac{1}{16}$ to $\frac{1}{12}$ in.) in diameter, are clearly visible. Although the beetle prefers sapwood (wood cut from the soft outer part of a tree trunk), it will also go for heartwood (the inner part of a trunk).

Powder post beetle. Reddish-brown in colour, 7 mm. ($\frac{1}{4}$ in.) long and more slender than the furniture beetle, the powder post beetle has a shorter life cycle – about ten months – and, after the grub has pupated, the young beetle emerges through a flight hole 1 to 1·5 mm. ($\frac{1}{16}$ in.) in diameter. It attacks the sapwood only of certain wide-pored hardwoods with a 3 per cent starch content, and is often imported into a new house from a yard where the merchant's stock has not been pre-treated. It may occur in quite new wood block floors or hardwood panelling.

Death-watch beetle. Mottled brown and yellow and 7 mm. ($\frac{1}{4}$ in.) long. The grub bores from four and a half to ten years and feeds mostly upon the dead branches of trees and on structural timbers already affected by fungus. It is often found in hardwood roofs and oak timbers of old churches. Bats feed on the beetle. Perhaps that is why bats favour residence in a belfry! The flight holes are 3 or 4 mm. ($\frac{1}{8}$ in.) in diameter.

House long-horn beetle. There are nearly sixty species of long-horn beetle, the males of the most frequently encountered being about 7 mm. ($\frac{1}{4}$ in.) long and the females 25 mm. (1 in.). The body is hairy and greyish or brownish-black in colour, with two transverse marks on the wing cases and two eye-like spots at the top of the head. Its life cycle is about five years and flight holes are between 3 and 7 mm. ($\frac{1}{8}$ to $\frac{1}{4}$ in.) in diameter. As one long-horn beetle can do many times the damage of a common furniture beetle it is fortunate that it is at present found only in certain areas of Surrey. Why it is confined to this unlucky district is not known, and how long it will be before it extends its activities to other parts of the country is a matter for conjecture.

Wood-boring weevils. Two species of wood-boring weevil, almost always associated with wet rot, are increasing – especially in the London area. Their holes are ragged and both adults and grubs devour wood.

Termites are among the most destructive of wood-boring insects. They are mostly confined to tropical and subtropical countries, not Britain and the cooler parts of the world. They are sometimes called *white ants* because they have similar social habits, each caste (colony) having a king, queen, soldiers and workers. Different from woodworm insofar as young termites do not undergo metamorphosis, they resemble their parents at birth. Of the 1,800 different species some of the most common have their habitation in the ground, feeding on adjacent timber. They do enormous damage in parts of the United States, Australia and Africa and, for that reason, wood used in building in affected areas is specially treated. Timber buildings are often erected on brick or concrete stilts to cool the house and to keep the pest at bay. This is not always effective because although termites will not work in the light they can cross open spaces by constructing their own tunnel of earth and saliva.

Diagnosis and Treatment

Whenever you spring-clean, examine the undersides and backs of furniture and also the insides of drawers and drawer linings. Here the wood may not have been properly finished and its slightly rough surface makes an ideal nursery for the common furniture beetle. In addition to tell-tale holes, look out for little piles of wood dust (called frass), about 10 to 25 mm. ($\frac{1}{2}$ to 1 in.) across, and looking for all the world as though a spot of plaster had dripped and dried.

We have already intimated that the holes are exit holes; and you may think, as the fully grown beetle has departed, there is no need to bother any more. But this beetle will lay more eggs if it is not prevented. And you may be sure that if one beetle has come out there will be more grubs inside the wood which will pupate and come out later, increasing the internal damage and the number of exit holes. Beetles like to make their exit through a rough surface, but they can also bite their way out through the finished front of furniture and, as we have seen in the case of doors, through painted surfaces.

Modern woodworm-killing fluid* penetrates well into soft-woods but for hardwood furniture and joinery, extra penetration can be achieved by injecting it into some of the flight holes, using a specially made injector which has a nozzle designed to fit the holes. The injector is obtainable at hardware stores.

As these holes join up within the wood there is no need to inject every one. Attend to the largest at 80 to 100 mm. (3 or 4 in.) intervals. Often, when you squeeze the fluid into one hole it will spout out of another at some distance away, thus proving that they do indeed join. Give at least three squeezes of the container to each hole you inject. To make doubly sure, apply the fluid all over the outside with a paint brush as well, not forgetting inside drawers and bottoms of feet.

Now if you leave the treated holes as they are, the woodworm will be killed; but when next springtime comes round and you examine the furniture again it may be difficult to tell whether the holes have been treated or whether there has been a fresh outbreak. You can get over this difficulty by filling the insides and the backs of furniture with cellulose wood filler* and the outsides with wax polish of the right colour.

Before undertaking any redecorating, examine the woodwork of a room. A tell-tale hole in a picture rail will indicate that a beetle has climbed behind where rough wood adjoins the plaster wall, laid its eggs, and the new generation, after it has completed its fell work, has decided to take its leave through the front. The same thing can happen to a skirting board and window frame and also to the unpainted bottom edge of a door.

Structural Timbers

Woodworm holes point an inexorable finger of judgement directly at the criminal. Frass provides circumstantial evidence only. The piles of dust may not be those dropped by a grub. They may be just piles of dust or spots of plaster!

The presence of woodworm in the trim of a room or in furniture is easily detected by one or other of these pieces of evidence. Woodworm is bad enough here in all conscience, but not nearly so damaging as when discovered in your roofing timbers or floor joists where thousands of pounds of investment are at stake.

In the dark recesses of an attic it is difficult to see holes in a large expanse of timber, and a floor is usually covered with linoleum or carpet which provides a hideout.

It will pay you to spend an hour or so aloft with a powerful hand torch or electric lamp on a long lead, going over every rafter, tie, purlin and post, foot by foot, and marking the position of any holes with a piece of chalk. Then, when you have finished, you will be able to assess the total damage.

You can have this survey carried out free by wood preservation experts* who will quote you a price which can be settled on easy terms; and on completion of the work you will be handed a guarantee that the treated timbers are clear of infestation and that, if reinfestation occurs, a further treatment will be carried out free of charge. This guarantee is useful evidence that the house is sound should you ever wish to sell. There must obviously be a limit to a guarantee, so it is generally drawn up to cover twenty years. But when properly done, the job will probably last the lifetime of the building.

An insurance broker can provide a policy against attack, should your house not already be infested.

If you do the work yourself – and it is quite within the capabilities of a handyman – invest in a sprayer which you can buy at a garden shop or department store. Get the type that holds about 10 litres (2 gallons) of fluid in a plastic container having a pump handle and to which is joined a length of flexible hose. At the end of the hose is a long metal pipe bent at its nozzle end and fitted with a cock (for turning off and on). It will cost you four or five pounds; or you can hire it from your local builders' hire service, the address of which will be in the classified section of your telephone directory.

Whatever type of sprayer you use, make sure it ejects fluid – not fluid in an atomised form as is the case with a spray-gun used for painting.

Roughly estimate the amount of fluid you will require by measuring the surface. With a boarded roof, take the overall measurement and add twice the depth of a rafter multiplied by its length and by the number of rafters. If the roof is not boarded, add the width of a rafter to twice its depth; multiply by its length and by the number of rafters. Follow a similar procedure with the joists supporting the ceiling below. A litre of fluid will cover approximately 4 sq. metres (1 gallon to 200 sq. ft), and you can order it from a builders' merchant in large drums — very much cheaper this way than in small tins made up for the treatment of furniture.

Brush down all woodwork and remove fallen dust and cobwebs from between the ceiling joists with a vacuum cleaner, first picking up any nails or odd pieces of flex left behind by plumbers and electricians. Then spray the surfaces of every bit of timber you see. If you confine your activities only to those that are affected, a beetle may be in the process of laying its eggs on an untreated part.

With roofing timbers it is not necessary to inject the individual holes. Roof supports are generally of cellular softwood; and the fluid contains a penetrating oil. The principle here is not immediately to kill the grubs which will be farther in but to provide a toxic envelope. When they start to emerge, they will contact the poison and die. That is why every part of every timber should be treated!

You can, of course, brush on the fluid with a distemper brush, but this will take proportionately longer.

Follow the same procedure for all species of woodworm with the exception of the long-horn variety. We have seen that the flight holes of this grub are larger than those of the others. As a rule, the long-horn beetle does not burrow deeply; so what you have to do in this instance is to scrape back the wood until you reach a firm part. Then touch in with the fluid, using a paint brush, and finish off by spraying the whole surface.

If the timber being treated is load-bearing and you have to scrape back very far, reinforcement may be necessary, and this can be done by introducing an additional new member or nailing on a plank about one and a half times the thickness of the scraped-away part.

You may have no long boards for temporarily covering the joists to provide a footing while you are working. So cut a number of smaller ones, sufficient to cover three joists without overlap, and nail a lip of wood underneath at each end to engage with the two end joists – something after the idea of the temporary attachment to fit over a bath while work is being done on a bathroom ceiling (Fig. 18A). This will prevent the board from overlapping a joist and tilting if its end is trodden on. You won't want to put your foot through the ceiling!

A few snags will present themselves to you.

How can you spray the narrow laths to which the plaster of the ceiling below is keyed? The answer is that there is no need to. The overspray from the roof rafters will attend to these.

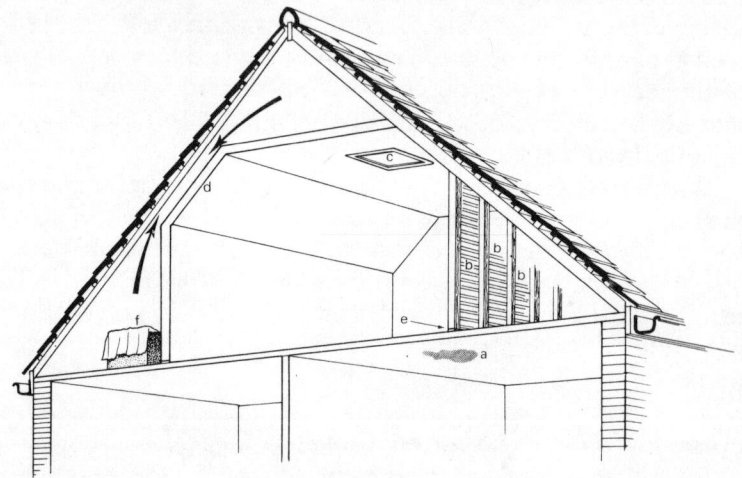

Fig. 25. Eradication of woodworm in an attic: (a) fluid penetrates plaster and stains ceiling; (b) laths of plastered wall relatively free of overspray; (c) trapdoor; (d) space between sloped ceiling and roof; (e) wooden plate in masonry; (f) tank protected by sheet

But, you may think, the fluid will penetrate the plaster and stain the ceiling (Fig. 25) at (a). To be on the safe side, use a quick-drying fluid which will not soak in so far. If you use the ordinary quality, which is better, leave the stain for a month to disperse by sideways penetration, and then cover it with two coats of aluminium primer sealer before redecorating with either paint or ceiling paper.

There will be little or no overspray on the laths of the plastered wall indicated by (b) in Fig. 25. These can be quickly treated with a small paintbrush.

The roof of the attic room shown in Fig. 25 presents a problem which is solved by cutting a rectangular hole in the ceiling between two joists. This will enable you to clamber up and spray. When finished, nail noggings from joist to joist at the extremities of the hole and fit a trapdoor, so that you may ascend again if necessary (c).

But how about the sloping part between ceiling and roof (d)? Here, working from above, insert the nozzle of the sprayer between the rafters as far down as you can go. Then, working from below, insert the nozzle as far up as you can go.

Fig. 25 shows a wooden plate partly buried in masonry (e). Spray the visible parts. Then bore 5 mm. ($\frac{1}{4}$ in.) holes down at an angle of about 45 degrees and inject fluid into them until they are full up.

Floors

Whenever you move a carpet during spring-cleaning, get down on your knees and examine the floor board by board. Carry out the same procedure before laying new linoleum.

If you come across any holes, lift the affected boards and spray the joists underneath, not forgetting all surfaces of the boards as well. You can use a brush if the outbreak is not extensive. After relaying the boards, inject the woodworm holes and fill with plaster or cellulose filler so that in future you will know what has been attended to.

In the event of a *small* outbreak you could provide a measure of protection for the *hitherto unaffected* joists without removing the boards, by boring two 5-mm. ($\frac{1}{4}$-in.) holes, one on each side of each board where it comes over a joist. Bore to nearly the depth of the joist and fill with woodworm fluid. The principle here is that the fluid will permeate the wood in both directions, thus disinfecting the interior of the wood. It will not, however, protect the outside by forming a toxic envelope.

With large outbreaks this would not be sufficient, and though you will have to treat the surface of timber throughout the room there is no need to take up every board. Prise up every fourth or fifth; then pass the nozzle of the sprayer underneath, between the joists.

We have already given a word of warning (page 31) about relaying floor covering immediately after a disinfestation job has been completed.

Precautions

Protect the lungs while spraying by wearing a mask. Cheap ones to cover nose and mouth may be purchased from a paint-shop or builders' merchant; or you can use a smog mask which can be bought from a chemist. While wearing such a contraption you will not be able to smoke. In any case, don't! If you want a rest and a 'draw' get right out of the enclosed space.

Protect the hands with barrier cream or wear an old pair of leather gloves, not rubber ones.

If there is a tank in the attic, cover it with a sheet (see Fig. 25 at (f)). Polystyrene lagging to a tank could be dissolved by the fluid, so drape the sheet over the sides as well.

Cover rubber electric cables with a sheet, or protect them with a coat of paint. Check that no wires are bare before you start spraying.

We must stress that a properly formulated woodworm fluid should be used. Paraffin and white spirit are certainly poisonous to the grub and beetle; but once these liquids have evaporated, their effectiveness ceases. Which means that you may momentarily discourage beetles from coming into your house and kill grubs and beetles about to 'surface', but you will not harm deeply buried grubs, nor will you prevent a further infestation. Fumigation is sometimes employed by means of a chemical candle giving off a poisonous smoke which settles on the surface of the wood; but this treatment is effective only for as long as the smoke deposit lasts and is only completely suitable for horizontal surfaces. Creosote partly does the job too but it does not permeate very deeply and tends to leach out. Then, of course, there is its stain and unpleasant odour to be considered.

What is wanted is a strong chemical with lasting properties, carried in an oil having the ability to penetrate; one that will kill grubs about to surface, one that will kill grubs in the depths of the wood when they surface at a later date, and one that will discourage beetles that fly after laying their eggs – in brief, a reliable woodworm fluid*.

If your home is affected, it is a hundred to one that adjacent houses also will have the trouble. Two people work more than twice as quickly as one; so get a neighbour to help you with your disinfestation and you can help him in return. Don't forget to examine the cupboard under the stairs and the cellar if there is one.

There is nothing particularly difficult about the work. What is needed is patience, perseverance, agility and old clothes which can be thrown away afterwards.

13
Simple
Electrical
Work

Do's and Don'ts

This chapter does not pretend to cover everything about the electric wiring of a house – a subject that would take a whole volume, or more than one, to cover fully. It just shows how you can put a minor fault right without always having to consult an expert. In any case, unless you have the necessary knowledge, you should periodically call in a qualified electrician to overhaul your wiring – say, every fifteen years.

Four things should be stressed straight away. First: don't experiment with electricity unless you know what you are doing. It is an excellent servant but a lethal master; and for this reason, in some parts of the world, Australia for instance, amateur electrical work is illegal. Second: never use any equipment that has a frayed or damaged flexible cable attached to it, particularly if the damage is where the cable is attached to the equipment or plug. Third: the use of electricity in damp situations considerably increases the risk of shock. Never carry a freestanding electric fire into a bathroom (see page 62), or use it in any other damp or steamy atmosphere. Fourth: be sure that the main switch is in the 'off' position before doing any repair work. Electricians often take chances with the main switch, but they are trained and know what risks they are taking.

Electricity enters your home through a consumer control unit which is generally housed in a box attached to one of the walls, and consists of a main switch and a number of fuses.

Alongside this will be a meter recording the amount of electricity consumed. In older houses there may be more than one set of main switches and fuse units; these will be dealt with later.

Definitions

Voltage is the measure of the pressure of electricity. Most electrical main supplies in the British Isles are at a pressure of 230, 240 or 250 volts AC (alternating current). Other countries may have different voltages and so foreign equipment may not necessarily be suitable for use in Britain.

Current is measured in amperes (amps) and indicates the rate of flow of electricity.

Power is measured in *watts*; 1,000 watts (W) = 1 kilowatt (kW), and depends both upon pressure and the rate of flow. This may be compared with water in a pipe, where the amount flowing out will depend both upon the bore of the pipe and the pressure behind the water.
So:

$$\text{Watts} = \text{volts} \times \text{amps}.$$

For example, a lamp marked on the bottom '240 volts, 60 watts' will pass a current of $\frac{60}{240}$ amps $= \frac{1}{4}$ amp, and an electric fire having a power of 2 kilowatts will pass a current of $8\frac{1}{3}$ amps when connected to a voltage of $240 \left(\dfrac{2{,}000 \text{ watts}}{240 \text{ volts}} = 8\frac{1}{3} \text{ amps} \right)$.

Unit is the name given to the amount of electricity used in one hour, and is also known as 1 kilowatt-hour (kWh).

Reading a Meter

You buy electricity from your local electricity board by the unit (kilowatt-hour) and the amount consumed is recorded on a meter.

Some meters can be read direct. The majority have a number

of clocks; and as these are connected behind by a series of cog wheels which engage with one another, one clock will work in one direction, its neighbour in the opposite direction, and so on.

To read a clock meter, start with the dial measuring 1,000 kilowatts (some start at 10,000), note where the hand is and take the reading next lowest to it. If it happens to be between 9 and 0, read it as 9. Do the same with the 100 kilowatt dial, and with the 10 and with the 1. You will see by this that the reading in Fig. 26A is 9,469 units.

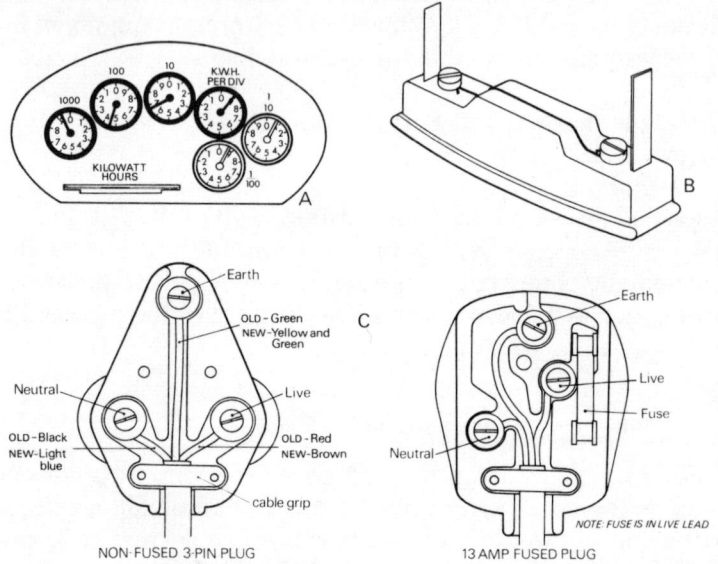

Fig. 26. A – Electric meter reading 9,469 units. B – Fuse. C – Non-fused 3-pin plug (left) and 13-amp fused plug with fuse in live lead (right)

The $\frac{1}{10}$ and $\frac{1}{100}$ clock faces may be ignored unless you are checking the cost of running a piece of electrical equipment.

To check equipment, make sure that all other outputs of current are turned off by seeing that the horizontal wheel, lower left in Fig. 26A, is stationary (the faster this wheel revolves the greater the amount of electricity is being used). Then connect the appliance to be tested. Take the meter reading before and after a specified time and multiply it by the cost of a unit of electricity which will be noted on your last bill.

A quicker way would be to examine the appliance to see the voltage and power – generally on a metal label riveted somewhere on the back. The cost now is:

Power in kilowatts × time in hours × price of a unit.

Or: power in watts ÷ 1,000 × time in hours × price of a unit.

Or: volts × amps ÷ 1,000 × time in hours × price of a unit.

Fuses

A fuse is a safeguard. Should a fault develop, causing a current to flow higher than that for which the cables have been designed, the fuse wire will melt and cut off the supply of electricity.

There are two kinds – those of wire joined to terminals in a small porcelain fuse holder and in which the wire can be replaced; and cartridge fuses which, when blown, have to be renewed with a fuse of the same rating.

The wire in the first kind, a typical one of which is shown in Fig. 26B, can melt, break or 'blow' through overloading or through the use of a faulty piece of electrical apparatus, or sometimes through ageing. To repair this type, switch off all electricity at the mains; then pull out each fuse holder from its socket in turn to see which one has a broken wire. When you have located it, replace the broken wire with a piece of the same gauge from a card of spare fuse wire previously purchased from an electrical shop.

Never use a heavier gauge of wire than that previously fitted, or the fuse will not provide the protection it is designed to give against overloading – which could cause a fire – or against faulty electrical equipment which could result in a fatal accident. Lighting requires a 5-amp fuse and power 15-amp.

If a fuse still blows when wire of the correct gauge has been fitted and provided that you are not overloading the circuit, then a fault exists in either the wiring or equipment; and this should be located and cleared by a qualified electrician.

Sometimes a device called a 'circuit breaker' takes the place of a fuse. This is manually operated and is also automatic in that, although it can be switched on and off by hand, it incorporates components that release the switch if the current exceeds a predetermined value, preventing its being reset by hand until the fault has been rectified.

Distribution

Old houses with one or two lighting circuits (all downstairs on one circuit, with a fuse in each wire, and all upstairs on a second circuit). Some have 5-amp sockets fitted on these circuits – cables, plugs and sockets being limited to a total current-carrying capacity of 5 amps. The sockets are intended for extra lamps and small appliances only.

With older houses having fuses in each wire it is possible to receive a shock from the lighting socket even if the bulb will not light and, apparently, there is no electricity to light it because one of the fuses has blown. For this reason, the main switch must be turned off before an attempt is made to work on any electrical circuit.

Modern houses. The shortcomings of the older systems have been eliminated by the provision of a fuse in each of the lighting circuits and by the use of 'ring main' circuits for all sockets. Each ring main, and there may be more than one, has one fuse only which, together with the main switch, is incorporated in a consumer's supply unit. The sockets are all of the same flat pin type and each has a maximum capacity of 13 amps.

With this form of house wiring, the main fuse is unlikely to blow, since it is of high capacity, generally 30 amp, and is provided to protect the main wiring. There is an individual fuse inside each plug which will blow if a fault develops in an appliance or in its flexible cable. It is essential that the rating of the fuse fitted inside these plugs is of capacity appropriate to the current consumption of the appliance. If it is not, the fuse will provide no protection to you and your property. Plugs of 13 amps are fitted with 13-amp fuses, suitable for an electric fire or heavy current appliance, and the fuse should be changed if it is intended for anything less – say, a reading lamp, radio or television.

The following will serve as a guide (but manufacturers' instruction leaflets should be studied in case they specify other-wise):

Clocks, lamps, electric razors, radio and television equip-ment, electric blankets and small soldering irons: 3 amp (brown) to BS 1362.

Electric fires, irons, drills and larger soldering irons: 13-amp (blue) to BS 1362.

If a 13-amp fuse were fitted to the plug of a table lamp, a fault in the lamp could cause up to 13 amps of electric current to flow along the flex which may be capable of carrying only 5 amps. The flex would get red hot – resulting in a fire.

Cartridge fuses for flat pin plugs are available in 3- or 13-amp ratings, the 3-amp being suitable for appliances up to 720 watts on 240-volt supplies, and 13-amp fuses for those up to 3,000 watts (3 kW).

You cannot always see a fault in such a fuse. You will have to fit a new one and try it out.

Adaptors

Adaptors, giving more than one outlet to the one socket, are very handy; but they should be used with caution. Some elec-trical experts damn them completely. It is so easy to overload the wiring if you do not know whether the cable running behind the skirting board or under the floor will carry the current you are using.

Tracing Faults

If your light suddenly fails, first test that it is not merely the bulb that has burned out and, at the same time, see that the switch is working properly. Then examine the fuse.

Where the system is one of individual fuse-holders, label the holders or draw up a plan showing which serves what and you will save a lot of time, for you will be able to go to the faulty unit straight away. An additional time-saver would be to have a number of spare fuses with different gauges of wire made up in advance.

The wire in a fuse-holder is secured by a terminal at each end (Fig. 26B). Make sure that you don't stretch it when tightening up the terminals. This you can do by winding one end of the wire round the first terminal in a clockwise direction and the other end round the second terminal in a counter-clockwise direction.

If the relevant fuse is in order, and it is a fire or electric iron that has gone dead, the fault may be in the plug or in the appliance.

Unscrew the cover and see that the two or three wires it houses are secure to the terminals. Sometimes they break or pull out when a cable is stretched too much. Pare the sheathing off the ends of the wires to a distance of 15 to 20 mm. ($\frac{1}{2}$ to $\frac{3}{4}$ in.) with a sharp knife. Twist the strands of each wire between your fingers and bend the ends over to make a neat connection without leaving any strands loose to touch the wrong terminals. Then reinsert in the terminals.

In old installations, the green wire is 'earth', the red is the live conductor and the black is neutral. In modern plugs a yellow and green wire is 'earth', a brown is the live conductor and light blue is neutral.

Make sure that the wires are connected to the correct terminals (Fig. 26C); and for safety's sake allow a little play for the earth wire so that, if the flex is accidentally pulled out, it will take the strain and not the cable. See that the cable grip (Fig. 26C) is tightly secured.

A flex leading out of the hole in an old-fashioned ceiling rose is generally wedged or knotted within the rose so that the weight of the glass shade does not place undue strain on the connections. With modern bayonet bulb-holders, the weight is taken by slots or holes in a small partition within the fitting and through which the wires are threaded. Before taking apart, note which wire runs through which slot or hole and route your new wiring in the same way.

In old houses, the flex could be of rubber or cotton, and this may have disintegrated, perhaps at the entry of a cable into a bayonet-type bulb-holder or where a flex suspended from a ceiling has become brittle through rising heat from the lamp underneath. Disintegration may also occur where the flex passes through a hole in an appliance – the covering may be intact but the buried wire broken. When renewing, use a plastic-covered flex of the same size, and don't forget to screw the grip back firmly. Plastic will not deteriorate so quickly under heat.

Nuts or screws may be loose inside a plug, bulb-holder, ceiling rose or appliance, and this will most likely produce an intermittent fault – one where an appliance works at times and not at others. A plunger inside a bayonet bulb-holder may be sticking or the spring broken, in which case the remedy is to buy a new bulb-holder. A new switch will be required if it houses broken springs or contacts.

The earliest bakelite bulb-holders tended to become distorted with heat. That is why it was often difficult to unscrew them to remove a lampshade. The fault does not happen these days unless a bulb of extra high wattage is used.

Flexible cables joining a piece of electrical equipment to a plug which, in turn, fits into a socket, should not be overlong or they will loop and wind across a floor to be tripped over. When an extension cable is required for use with workshop appliances or lawnmowers, use the heavy three-core flexible type, with resilient plugs and sockets to withstand rough handling. When adding to the length of a cable, make sure that the cable-to-cable connector has a retaining device to prevent its being pulled apart.

A final warning: appliances fitted with a three-core cable should never be used with a bayonet-type two-pin plug connecting live and neutral wires only. This is dangerous. Certain modern pieces of equipment, however, are specially *double-insulated* for use from bulb sockets. Information on this point will be given in the manufacturer's leaflet.

14
Simple
Plumbing

The Basic Plumbing System

Dedicated do-it-yourselfers may have the ability to fit in new cisterns, install central heating and alter the pipe layout of their homes – but that hardly comes within the scope of a book on home *maintenance*. We shall deal here solely with repairs that can be carried out by anybody using quite ordinary tools.

First, get to know your plumbing system and you will be able to deal with small problems with full knowledge of what you are doing. Your system will follow the pattern of that shown in Fig. 27, though it may vary slightly from house to house.

Water enters from the street through a pipe buried well below ground level. There will be a cock at (a), probably in the pavement outside, which can be reached by lifting a small metal cover and using a long-handled key-shaped tool something like a box spanner. You can make such a tool yourself by cutting grooves in the end of a length of metal pipe and fitting a handle at the other end comprising a wooden rod passing through holes bored at each side, as is shown in Fig. 27. This cock is normally used by the Water Board only in cases where the whole water supply to the house needs to be cut off, including the entry pipe.

Coming up through the foundations and floorboards the pipe

will have another cock (b), generally under the kitchen sink where it can be easily reached. Above that will be the cold water tap (c). This is where you should draw your drinking water – not from taps serving water stored in cisterns that may become contaminated. There may or may not be more taps serving clean water from the mains. You can find out for yourself if there is one, say, in the bathroom by seeing if cock (b) turns the supply off at that point almost immediately.

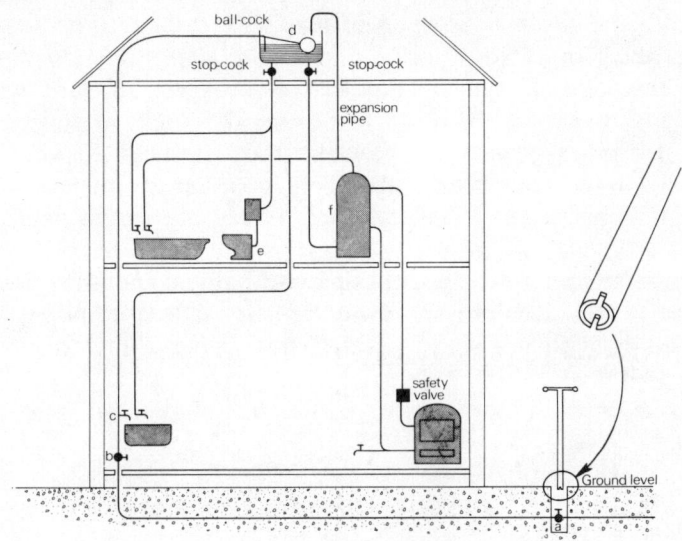

Fig. 27. Pipe layout

The water is now forced by pressure to a storage cistern (d) in the roof. From this will flow cold water (not intended for drinking) to washbasin, bath and w.c. cistern (e).

Another pipe descends to fill the supply to the storage cylinder (f), and from this the water flows to whatever source of heat there is – a fire or boiler. As water expands on being heated, it rises back and, being light, tends to lie on top. That is why you can often draw hot water soon after a fire is lit – but the amount may be small. If it is left for a few hours the heat will gradually warm up the whole contents of the cylinder.

From the top of the cylinder run pipes connecting the hot water supply to bathroom and kitchen.

Frost Precautions

In severely cold weather, damage is done to a pipe not when entrapped ice thaws but during the actual freezing process, because water expands on solidifying with a force so great that it bursts the pipe. The burst may not be noticed until warmer weather turns the solid ice back into liquid form.

The pipe bringing water to your house should be at least three-quarters of a metre (2 ft 6 in.) below ground level and so beneath the reach of frost. And it is wise to have it protected under the ground floor until it reaches the main stopcock. After that the general run of builders don't seem to care what happens, and it will be up to you to see that tanks are lagged*, and also pipes – particularly where they run near a roof. Obviously if the cold water pipes run in or on an internal wall they will be better protected than if they are on an external wall.

Outlets from sinks, washbasins and baths sometimes freeze so that water does not run away. It is of little use bailing out and filling with hot water because this, being lighter than the cold, will float on top. You will have to go outside and pour hot water over the pipe where it comes out of the wall into the open.

To guard against such freezing in severe weather, see that taps are turned off properly. Drips running down the pipe will

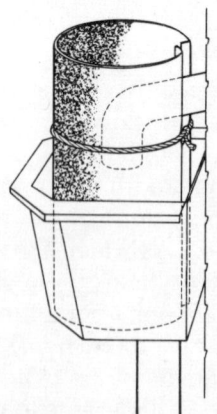

Fig. 28. Protection for outlet pipe to hopper

quickly freeze and more drips following them will solidify even more quickly until they build up sufficiently to close the orifice.

Bathroom waste pipes leading into a hopper on an outside wall in an exposed position, where a bitter north wind whips against them unobstructed by other buildings, can cause continuous trouble. Build a wind barrier with a small piece of roofing felt curved round inside the hopper and tie it round the pipe so that it does not blow away (Fig. 28).

If a pipe bursts, turn the water off at the mains and drain the pipe. Then you can make a temporary repair until a plumber arrives by screwing a special clip, obtainable at a hardware store, over the fault or by applying plastic metal* to the edges of the crack and squeezing them together with pliers. Plastic pipes may be temporarily repaired by applying a hot soldering iron to the break.

Tap Washers

A dripping tap is a source of annoyance and leads to waste of water and to stains in sink, washbasin and bath.

If it is the kitchen cold tap that has gone wrong you can shut off the water supply at point (b) shown in Fig. 27, while you replace the washer. Turn on the tap and it will take only a few seconds to empty the pipe. If a bathroom cold tap draws water from the storage cistern, shut off (b) and run off water until the cistern is drained. This may take five or ten minutes. If a washer has gone in any of the hot taps, and where there is no intervening stopcock to cut off the supply, put out the fire and drain both hot and cold cisterns.

Now you can get to work.

Insert the plug in the sink, basin or bath, so that screws will not get lost down the waste pipe if dropped. Turn the tap to the 'on' position and unscrew the shroud (Fig. 29) where there is one. If this has become corroded, use mole grips, protecting the chromium with a piece of cloth; or you can use a jubilee-type clip, or another way is to wind stout cord round it and form a tourniquet with a long nail; when tightened this should be sufficient to move the most obstinate of screw threads.

Under the shroud will be a large nut. This may have a left- or right-handed thread; so go cautiously with a spanner until you find out. Don't touch the gland nut above it.

Support the pipe with one hand while you loosen the large nut with the other — otherwise the pipe may twist. The whole tap will now come off revealing a jumper loosely attached and holding a washer.

Remove the retaining nut and renew the washer. Before replacing the parts smear the threads with Vaseline to make removal at a future date easier.

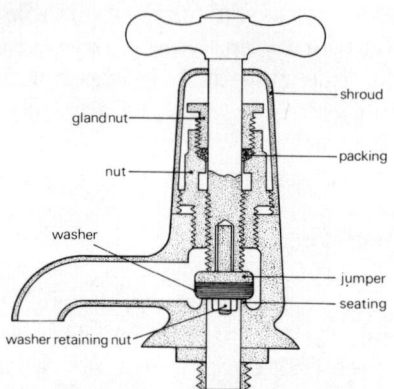

Fig. 29. Tap construction

If this does not do the trick, the valve seating on which the washer engages may be dirty. Clean it round with your finger or a small brush. Or it may be worn — in which case you can buy new plastic seatings to fit; or you can get a plumber to regrind the old seating.

The 'Supatap'* is designed so that a faulty washer can be replaced without turning off the water supply — because a check valve is incorporated which comes into action when the tap is slackened.

The gland nut, which should not be touched when only the washer has gone wrong, covers a small chamber containing hemp or cotton packing saturated in wax or grease. This packing may become dry through detergent dropping down inside; and when this happens water will ooze out through the top when the tap is turned on. Tightening the nut slightly will often cure the trouble, though it will subsequently make the taps stiffer to turn on and off. Eventually the packing will have to be replaced – which is quite an easy job.

Ballvalves

Water storage tanks and w.c. cisterns are supplied by an inlet pipe; and quite obviously they would overflow if there were not some device for automatically turning off the water when it reaches a prescribed height.

This device is generally a ballcock, consisting of a copper or plastic ball into which one end of a metal arm is screwed. The other end of the arm engages with a piston which slides in and out of a short piece of tubing fitted with a seating and screwed on to the inlet pipe. The piston has a washer at one end forming a valve. (See Fig. 30.)

When the tank or cistern is empty, the ball rests on the bottom and this opens the valve to let the water in. As the water rises, so does the ball, gradually sliding the piston farther along the tube until the washer rests on the seating.

At this point the water is shut off.

Pistons that run horizontally are known as 'Portsmouth'. Those that run vertically are called 'Croydon'. (See Fig. 30A and C.) There is another type consisting of a diaphragm, which works on very much the same principle.

Supposing something goes wrong with a Portsmouth or Croydon mechanism, the inlet pipe will fail to shut off and the ball will continue to rise until a safety outlet is reached when the water will overflow into another pipe let into an outside wall. This prevents the house from becoming flooded. The danger of allowing this overflow pipe to continue discharging over a long period has already been dealt with on page 78.

There is nothing difficult in putting the fault right, though it must be admitted that you may have to be a bit of a contortionist to reach some cisterns in some attics. Turn the water off and take out the split pin to release the ballcock arm which is attached to the piston. This means straightening the pin and tapping its end gently until you can get pliers to work. The arm and ball can now be removed.

If the ball is punctured it will be full of water, and will not rise. Renew the ball.

If the ball does not require renewal, check the arm. It may be set at too high an angle so that the ball does not shut off the valve until the water reaches a height above the outlet. The arm is easily bent if you take it out and use a hand at both ends. But do the bending gradually and by trial and error, as very little correction will be needed.

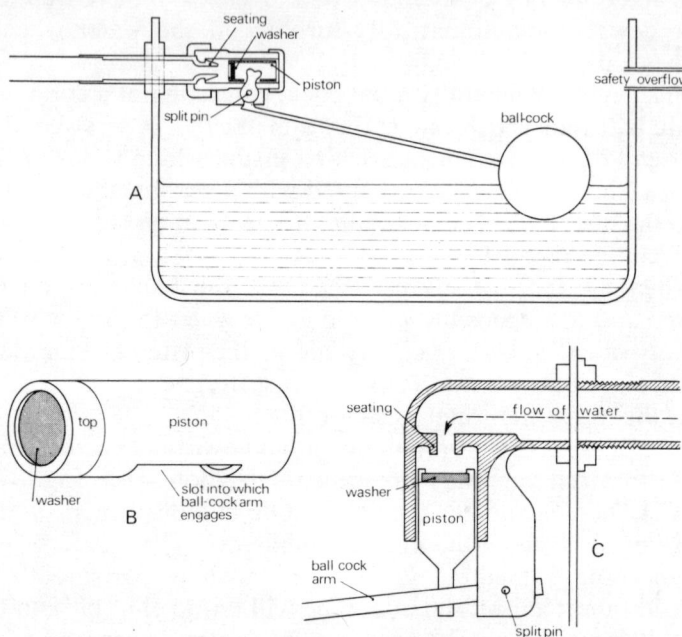

Fig. 30. A – Cistern and ballcock with Portsmouth-type piston. B – Portsmouth-type piston. C – Ballcock with Croydon-type piston

Assuming ball and arm are OK, the next thing is to take out the piston. You may have to employ a piece of bent wire to do this. Be careful not to injure the surface of the piston.

You will see that at the end of the piston is a rubber or composition washer kept in place by a screwed-on top (see Fig. 30B). As this fitting is extremely precise, you may not at first detect the join between the top and the body.

Hold the top (or washer end) of the piston tightly in a vice or mole grips, protecting it with cloth, put a screwdriver into the slot farther down and turn. Pick out the old washer and renew. Before rescrewing on the top, smear the thread with Vaseline. Clean the surface of the piston, taking care not to scour it, and smear that also with Vaseline – not too much or you may cause 'water hammer' (see below).

If, after carrying out all this, the ballcock still fails to function, call in a plumber to replace the fitment.

It is not suggested that you have a spare ball for an emergency but you can keep one or two spare washers.

Suppose a fault occurs when all the shops are shut and you have no spares, you can shake water out of a leaky ball and cover the fault with Sellotape or stick on a tyre patch. A temporary washer may be made out of a sheet of rubber or from one or two pieces of a motor tyre built up to the required thickness.

There are high- and low-pressure valves, and if the wrong one is fitted there may be long fill-up periods.

Water Hammer

Do your pipes beat out an unwelcome tattoo every time you turn off a tap? If so, they may be subjected to hydraulic pressure in excess of normal and you should attend to them because a great strain is being imposed upon the system which might result in leakage at joints. The first weakness to look for is in the main cock (Fig. 27) at (b). Is water entering the house at too high a pressure? Then try turning the cock down a bit. If this does not do the trick, examine tap washers. If they are too 'springy' or have 'spread', as is sometimes the case with old ones made of rubber, they should be replaced. Then examine ball valves to see if they 'chatter' when water is flowing into a cistern. If the trouble persists after washers have been renewed, look inside the cistern and see if there is a downpipe fitted to the valve, the other end being below the surface of the water. If there is not, get one fitted. It will also quieten the refill. A temporary remedy is to tie a colander under the ball and it will lessen the formation of ripples on the surface of the water.

In hot water installations, air entrapped in the pipes can

cause trouble. Here you may have to get the pipes realigned so that they slope sufficiently for air to rise and be expelled through the expansion pipe. Or a sharp bend in a pipe may have to be straightened slightly. The expansion pipe (see Fig. 27) could be of too small an internal diameter and may need replacing with a larger one. Or the pipe could be attached to the tank by back-nuts – in which case a plumber might think it advisable to replace them with a flanged connection to compensate for shudder.

Blocked Sinks

Buy a plunger for keeping sink waste pipes clear. This takes the form of a hollow rubber cone fitted to the end of a handle. See that the handle and cone are about half a metre (18 in.) long.

At the side or top of the sink you will find an orifice which prevents overflowing should a tap inadvertently be left running. Stuff a piece of cloth into this to seal it. Put the plunger over the drain, turn on the cold tap and plunge up and down vigorously. Don't use half-hearted measures. Force is required. When this does not clear the stoppage, unscrew a nut which you will see at the bottom of the U-pipe under the sink and poke out the obstruction with bent wire.

If these two methods fail, call in a plumber who will bring clearing canes and 'ferrets' with him.

Drains

In all probability the drainage of your house – sinks, baths and w.c.s – will be carried to outside 100-mm. (4-in.) pipes laid to a gradient of 1 in 40 at a depth of about 1·25 m. (4 ft), each length of pipe being joined to the next length with a socket.

At each bend in the pipe system will be an inspection chamber, 0·5 × 1 m. (3 ft × 1 ft 6 in.), with an iron cover. Additional inspection chambers may also be fitted to a straight run of pipe if it is long. Chambers are fitted with means of ventilation.

Sometimes rain collecting on the surface of the ground and

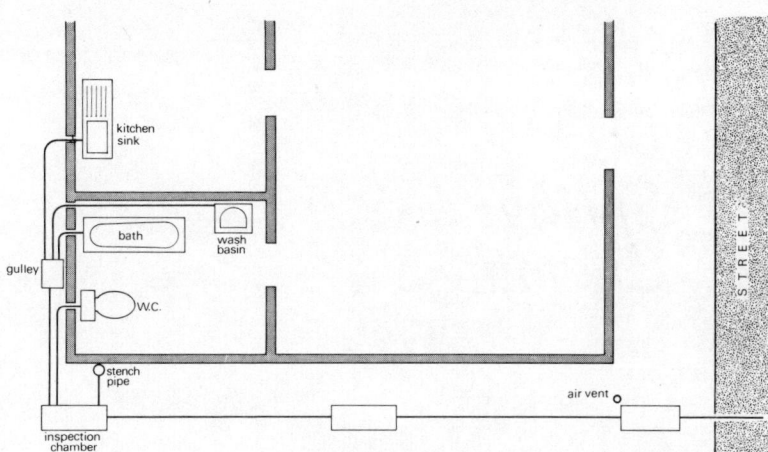

Fig. 31 Drainage layout

from roofs is channelled into the house drainage system and at other times it flows into a separate system. Fig. 31 shows a typical separate system. The part beyond the inspection chamber nearest to the street should not be interfered with. It is the responsibility of your local authority.

Waste flows from the kitchen sink, bath and washbasin into a gully which must be kept clear. Remove the grid of the gully periodically and brush off loose hair and vegetable waste that may have collected. Put your hand down the U-pipe and fish out any solid matter which may be too heavy for the flow of water to carry away. The w.c. outlet runs straight to the nearest inspection chamber.

If water still rises in the gully after the pipe has been cleared, lift the covers of the inspection chambers one by one to locate the obstruction. It may be that the roots of a privet hedge have pushed through and are causing a blockage. If so, cut them away and reline the chamber with a one-of-cement-and-two-of-sand mortar. When giving a test flushing, colour the water with permanganate of potash crystals so that you can trace its progress through the pipe system.

15
Spring Cleaning

When the first spring sun starts to show up dilapidations is the time to take stock and see what needs doing to keep the home in a good state of appearance and preservation.

A cursory glance at a room or at the outside paintwork will reveal little except that it is getting a bit shabby. When you come to spring-clean, however, concentrate your eyes on the surface, a square foot at a time, and you cannot fail to note the extent of wear and damage. This is perhaps the biggest advantage of an annual 'turn-out'. It supplies a physical balance sheet showing the current structural state of your property, and it is then up to you to turn a deterioration 'loss' into a restoration 'profit'.

You may decide that the kitchen wants completely redecorating. The dining room has one or two greasy marks on the walls and the paint on the windows is starting to peel — otherwise the room is sound and, apart from a touch-up here and there, will be all right for at least another year. Just because the window sashes show signs of wear does not necessarily mean that the whole room needs redecorating. You can roll back the carpet, lay old bedsheets or newspapers on the floor and attend to this bit of paintwork and nothing else.

Out of doors, the side of the house facing the greatest amount of sun may have started to go. If the other sides are in fair condition why re-do all round? You may think the difference between new and old paint will show; but passers-by cannot see all four sides of a detached house at once – or the three sides of one that is semi-detached, or the front and back of a terrace house.

Try and programme all your maintenance work so that the minimum amount of time is devoted to keeping the house in tip-top condition. For instance, with the assumptions just made, a week of your spare time may be needed to repaint the kitchen, one week for painting one side of the exterior, and half a week for touching up the dining room.

The Annual Clean

A housewife may wonder why the best part of a chapter of this book needs to be devoted to such a simple subject as removal of dirt. Surely all that has to be done is to pour soapless detergent into warm water and wash the dirt off? But if she understands exactly what dirt is, she will make a greater success of the job and save on expensive cleaning materials. Tons of washing powders are wasted every year by people thoughtlessly tipping into water the contents of a packet. Detergents act only to a certain limit, and using more than is necessary is just a waste of money.

The kind of dirt mostly encountered in houses is composed of minute solid particles held together by an oily film. The oily film may only be grease from the hand, what we call finger-marks. The finer the solid particles the more difficult they will be to remove because they cling together, whereas larger particles will break apart.

To remove dirt quickly and effectively, the oily film has to be broken; and this is best done by wetting, emulsifying and saponifying.

With simple wetting, water will tend to lie on top of grease. By emulsifying the grease you get the water behind it, as it were. Emulsifying means breaking the surface into tiny globules, and saponifying means combining alkalis with oily deposits to form a crude soap which is soluble in water.

If you rub hard and for long enough you can clean almost any surface with cold water and nothing else. By adding a chemical cleanser you speed up the process by breaking down the grease. And if the water is warm, not only will the wetting action be assisted but the heat will partially melt the grease and make it more vulnerable to the action of the cleanser.

Common sense may suggest your starting at the top of a wall and washing downwards. But common sense is not always right; and if you do this, trickles of the cleansing solution will flow onto the dry surface beneath, leaving streaks that will be difficult to remove. Forming in droplets, they may also have a concentrated effect in patches and may weaken that part of the surface.

Therefore, whatever cleansing materials you use, start at the bottom and work up, so that trickles will run down onto an already wetted surface where they will become diluted and disperse. Then you can swill the surface with clean water, this time starting from the top.

With *very* dirty patches, leave the cleanser on for a few minutes for the chemical action to be completed; but don't allow the surface to dry out completely or you will have to go to all the trouble of rewetting it. Then remove the cleanser with water and apply more. This will do the job safely and efficiently. If you use one lot of cleanser only, with extra strength, you may cause damage; and the material will certainly be weakened and rendered less effective because it will have become adulterated with grease.

A woman washing her hair will use a little shampoo to start the emulsifying process, then swill it off and apply a second lot to complete the job. A man using an old-fashioned shaving brush will know that the time needed for his beard to soak before using the razor will be lessened if he swills the first lot of soap off and gives his chin a second application. Why not, then, adopt a similar principle with a dirty wall or door?

Of course, the paintwork would have to be in a pretty bad state to justify this seemingly double operation.

All cleansing solutions should be removed, in spite of what some manufacturers say to the contrary. If you leave them on they might have a deleterious effect – perhaps only slight – on the existing decoration, and if you propose to redecorate you will leave behind a fine film which could affect adhesion of new wallpaper. In the case of paint, cleansing solutions *could* mingle with the components and upset the formulation. They could also 'bleed' through the decoration to cause stains.

When removing the cleansing solution, change the water frequently. By using dirty water you will be taking off one lot of dirt and depositing another. Keep turning the cloth so that you will not rub the dirt back in. Then mop over the surface with a squeezed-out cloth or sponge.

We have just spilled an ink bottle over the manuscript of this chapter. To remove the puddle of ink, we used a dampened piece of blotting paper. Because the blotting paper was already slightly damp it attracted the liquid ink and soaked it up more quickly than a dry piece would have done. For the same reason, a damp cloth (not wringing wet but squeezed out as tightly as possible) will remove water from the surface more efficiently than will a dry cloth. But don't bunch up the cloth when using it; open it out flat and you will dry the surface more quickly and more evenly. If any smears are left, go over the surface again with an absorbent dry cloth. Don't rub too vigorously on a matt-painted surface or you will *polish* it, and this will cause 'sheariness'.

Following this method, gloss paint is very easy to clean. A matt surface is more difficult. Having minute crevices it holds the dirt more tenaciously and a greater friction is set up between the surface and cloth. Then again, although emulsion paint can be scrubbed, you should go steady with the water, because the moisture will soak in and weaken the adhesion of the coating.

Water-paint, sometimes called washable or oil-bound distemper, can be washed with a minimum of water, but it cannot be scrubbed. If you attempt to wash *non-washable* or size-bound distemper even lightly, you will remove it — which means that you will have all the trouble of applying another coat.

It is always better to remove a dirty patch soon after it appears. The chemicals in the dirt will not have a chance of biting into the surface and making removal difficult.

If there is a small mark on an emulsion-painted wall, that will not come off by ordinary cleaning, rub it vigorously with a domestic scouring powder. This may leave an obviously light spot which will look almost as bad as the dirt. So when you have removed the spot, apply a clean damp cloth and, starting at about a foot or so away, rub lightly, following a decreasing circular motion and applying more pressure as you go, until you reach the cleaned mark. This will 'feather off' the difference in tone, so that it will be less obvious.

Before starting to clean or redecorate a room, carry out any repairs necessary. The check list at the end of this chapter will help you here.

You won't want to remove linoleum before washing down the walls of a room, and you cannot very well take up composition tiles. If splashes of the cleansing solution being used are allowed to form in puddles and dry out, the floor covering will look as though it has broken out in a rash. So protect it with a dust sheet. Linoleum can be given a good coat of wax polish — but not vinyl floor covering.

Vinyl and other washable wall coverings are easy to clean. Ordinary wallpaper can be dealt with by lightly brushing with a clean soft banister brush. If really bad, rub with stale bread; and if this does not do the trick, wipe over ever so gently with a sponge dipped in diluted Stergene and squeezed out. Two measures to a bowl of water is ample.

Cleaning Metal Surfaces

Dirt is not only held to metal surfaces by an oily film; it may also stick by electrostatic attraction. And sometimes corrosion products combine with the dirt to seal it in.

All traces of corrosion must therefore be removed — not only because of the damage it does to the substrate and paint-film, but because you cannot remove all the dirt without taking off the corrosion.

Many people paint over rust because, they say, the paint sticks so well. It does — for a time. But when iron rusts, the resulting iron oxide increases in volume. In expanding it causes the paint to peel off. Rust also will spread under an otherwise sound paintfilm and the peeling action will continue with it.

You can deal with rust either by chipping with a hammer, scraping, wirebrushing or rubbing with emery cloth, or by a combination of all four, preferably with the help of a rust solvent* or phosphating material.

Cleaning and renovating furniture is dealt with in Chapter 16.

Windows

Professional window-cleaners use scrim, a coarse absorbent linen, and plain water for their work. You will notice how they rinse the scrim frequently and wring it out – because the cleaner it is, the quicker it will do the work.

Many people add methylated spirit to warm water – an excellent idea, because the spirit dissolves grease. But we have found that the quickest way is to wipe the pane quickly over with a coarse, wringing-wet cloth to remove most of the dirt, and then, while the surface is still wet, go over it with crumpled newspaper. The absorbent paper dissolves grease and the printer's ink leaves a polish on the surface. When dry, dust quickly with a clean cloth to remove any flecks.

Some water may get onto the sashes; but a brisk wipe round with another cloth will keep these clean – a job that few window-cleaners will do. The white powder that collects on aluminium window sashes can be removed with fine wire wool, Brillo pads or chromium cleaner.

Outside Work

An annual clean of outside decoration will remove industrial deposits which bite in, dust which abrades, chalking (paint pigment denuded of its medium) which dulls the gloss, and efflorescence which stains. If you live near the sea, washing down will take off salt which has a bleaching effect on paint. Salt is also hygroscopic; that is to say, it attracts moisture. If a damp salty atmosphere seeps through a crack in the paint, it will cause moisture to form behind the film, and this will result in flaking.

But not all dirt is destructive to paint. Provided its acid content is not too high, it will actually protect the paintfilm because it forms a barrier to the ultra-violet rays of the sun. What a lovely excuse for postponing cleaning the outside of a house! But then, appearances must be considered.

Outside cleaning cannot be done so meticulously as inside. In the case of the painted rendering of a wall you are most likely to be tempted to leave it as it is. But if you are per-nickety, get somebody to hose it down while you wield a long handled broom – protecting yourself with a mackintosh, or you will get as wet as the wall!

Check List

Before starting to spring clean or repaint:

1. Nail down loose floorboards (Chapter 4).
2. Ease sticking windows (Chapter 7).
3. See that doors fit properly; oil locks and hinges and adjust if necessary. Renew draught excluders (Chapter 6).
4. Replace faulty tap washers (Chapter 14).
5. Sweep chimneys. Replace broken hearth tiles (Chapter 5).
6. Examine electric light fittings and see that they function properly (Pages 105–7).
7. Examine woodwork, particularly picture rails and floor-boards, for woodworm holes; but don't treat them *before* painting or the paint may not adhere properly (Chapter 12).
8. Replace broken handles on drawers and cupboards of fitted furniture. Renew runners if necessary.
9. Outside: clear out rainwater gutters and check that they are in order (Chapter 1).

16
Furniture
Renovation

Some Basic Principles

If you cannot steady wobbly furniture by tightening retaining screws you will have to add metal angle brackets underneath where they will not be seen, or small blocks of wood glued to the loose joints – also from underneath. When screws no longer hold, fill holes with asbestos filler* or decrease their size with wall plugs*; or you may be able to drive larger-size screws in without using plugs.

Where two planes of one piece of furniture are fastened at right-angles and secured by blocks of wood, the blocks often fall off with age or misuse. Clean off the old glue by scraping and sanding and re-attach with fresh glue, clamping the joint tightly until set.

When gluing in a new piece to replace a broken part of a surface that will be seen, choose wood of the same grain texture and arrange so that the grain of the new and old run in the same direction. Peeling veneer should be attended to by regluing before the trouble spreads. If the veneered piece has broken off and become lost, a timber shop will match it up and you can then apply the new veneer with the grain running in the same direction as the surroundings.

Chairs

Loose chair rails should be pulled apart, scraped clean and reinserted after coating with fresh glue. Give added security by pinning, or make a tourniquet of string tightened with a piece of dowelling until the joint has set, as is shown in Fig. 32 (top).

Rush- or cane-bottomed chairs can be reseated with new rushes or canes or their substitutes which can be obtained

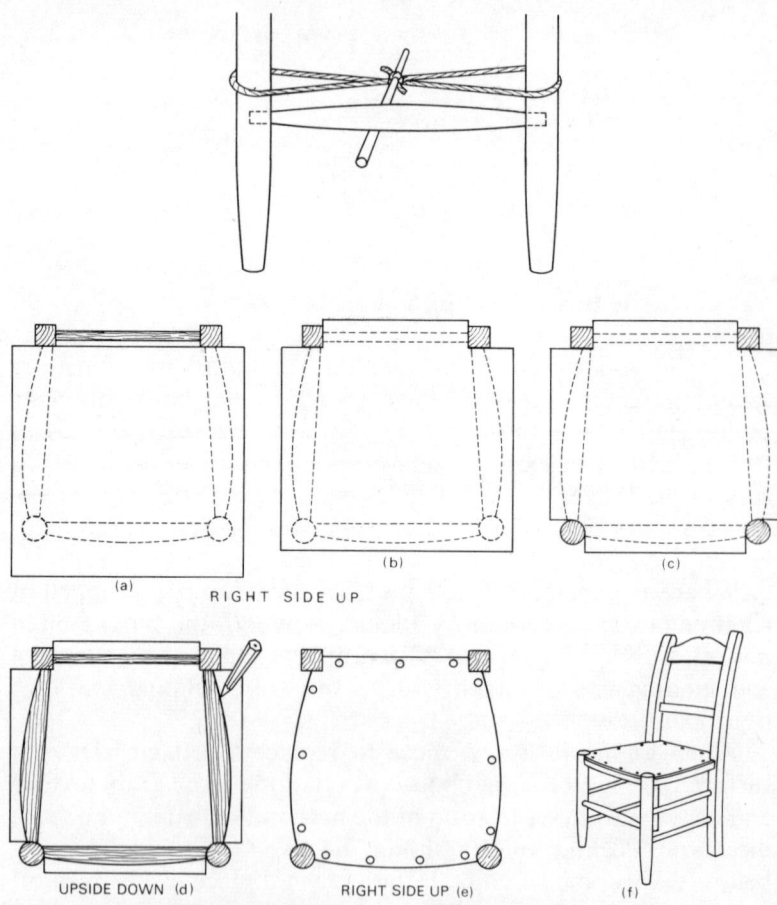

RIGHT SIDE UP

(a)   (b)   (c)

UPSIDE DOWN (d)   RIGHT SIDE UP (e)   (f)

Fig. 32. Top – To repair chair rail, glue rail and secure by string tourniquet until glue dries. Foot – Procedure for reseating a kitchen chair with plywood.

in lengths for do-it-yourself weaving or in sheets already woven*.

If the chairs are intended for a kitchen, you may think it more sanitary to reseat them with three-ply (3.2-mm. plywood).

Cut the rush all round just inside the framework of the seat with a pad saw and the centre will fall out. The sides can then be unwound after tacks have been removed.

Lay a sheet of cardboard, slightly oversize, on the seat and mark the position of the back legs (Fig. 32) at (a). Cut out their shape and replace the cardboard so that it fits, with the back overlapping the back of the frame (b). Mark the position of the front legs and cut these out (c). This particular cutting will have to be done more or less by trial and error – so a card template is necessary before you work on the plywood. When you have achieved a perfect fit, secure temporarily with a few drawing pins.

Turn the chair over and trace the outline of the seat frame onto the back of the cardboard, leaving about 3 or 4 mm. ($\frac{1}{8}$ in.) overlapping (d). Remove and cut.

Trace the outline of the shaped card onto the face of the sheet of plywood and cut the plywood, which will now fit around the legs precisely, but will slightly overlap the edges. Turn the chair the right way up and secure this 'seat' to the frame with three copper, brass or decorated chair nails at the back, four at the front and three at each side, protecting the nail-heads while hammering with a block of wood (e). To prevent the wood from splitting, bore guide holes first. File and glasspaper the edges to come flush with the seat frame, and you will have the finished job (f).

After stripping the old rush seat, you may find that the four members of the seat frame may not be quite level. Underlay any low ones with strips of thin wood before attaching the seat. If a member is low at one end and level at the other, insert a short strip of wood to compensate for the low part and spread hard stopping or plastic wood* along to fill the slope. Nail on the seat while the stopping is still soft. If any exudes through the seat springing up and down under the blows of the hammer, knife it back in; then wipe off the surplus and leave to harden.

The seat may now be stained to match the remainder of the chair.

If you propose painting, the paint will cover the heads of the chair nails and spoil the look of them. So secure the cut plywood to the frame with lost-head pins, driving them in 3 or 4 mm ($\frac{1}{8}$ in.) away from the points where you propose inserting the chair nails. Trim up the seat and paint. When dry, drive in the chair nails – the heads of which will cover the indentations made by the lost-head pins.

Previously Painted Furniture

If you can manage to rub down a painted piece of furniture to destroy the old gloss and featheredge the 'step' surrounding the chipped parts at the same time, you can repaint with an alkyd resin paint* without removing all the old coating. Touch in bared parts with wood primer; then give two applications of an undercoat over the whole lot. Undercoat is highly pigmented and inclined to dry 'ropey', so lightly sand the second coat smooth with fine garnet paper, dust off, wipe over with a tack rag (cloth soaked in sticky non-drying varnish, obtainable from paintshops) and apply the finishing coat.

Alternatives are a polyurethane paint* which dries extra hard, or one of the paints sold in an aerosol pack*. Follow the manufacturer's directions for application. Aerosol paints are useful in achieving an 'olde worlde' vignetted effect at the edges of furniture.

Mouldings or high parts may be picked out in gold or silver paint on top of the finishing coat by a dry-brush process, consisting of dipping the brush into the paint, dragging it across the edge of the container to remove as much as possible, and then lightly brushing over reliefs.

Another way of getting reliefs in a different colour from that of valleys in a moulded surface is to paint the whole piece in the colour required for the high parts. Leave to dry, paint the whole piece again in the colour required for the valleys and, while this is still wet, wipe off the high parts with a non-fluffy cloth.

Porous woods may require filling before painting. Brush on a creamy consistency of cellulose filler* in the direction of the grain of the wood. Leave for ten minutes and wipe off across the grain. Sanding, using fine-grade abrasive paper (rubbed in the direction of the grain) may also be necessary.

Wicker Furniture

Dirty wicker furniture can seldom be restored by ordinary cleansing methods. So much pressure will be used on the scrubbing brush to reach the interstices that the finish may come off the raised parts. You will generally have to repaint after cleaning, applying a wood primer with a foam sponge and finishing with an aerosol packed paint*.

Peel back loose wicker to its point of firm attachment, apply glue to the exposed frame and replace.

Painting Previously Stained Furniture

Painting previously stained and polished furniture is not easy.

The polish must be removed with white spirit and wirewool, turning and renewing the wool frequently to prevent its 'spreading' the wax. If a silicone polish has been used – and most polishes these days contain silicones – it may be necessary to use silicone remover. Then you will have to take off the varnish and seal in the stain.

If you can determine what type of varnish it is, you can often take off polish and varnish at the same time. First try dry-scraping. If this does not achieve the required objective, use a non-caustic paint stripper*. A blow-lamp is not advised because it is so easy to char the wood, though you can minimise char marks by applying raw linseed oil and setting the coating alight with the blow-lamp. If you decide to follow this method, experiment on a waste piece of varnished wood first.

As stain soaks in, it cannot be removed completely without planing the surface. The solvents of paint applied on top will 'activate' old stain causing it to bleed through. You can, however, apply a proprietary sealer* or two coats of aluminium primer. When dry, sand down the second coat to remove nibs of paint, and apply two finishing coats on top. The sanding should be done lightly or you will rub through. As aluminium primer sealer has a filling action, undercoating is not necessary; but two finishing coats are – otherwise a dull silveriness will appear on the surface.

French polish can be removed with methylated spirit or cellulose thinner and fine wirewool.

Bleaching

Suppose you have a dark-stained piece of oak which you would like to change to a lighter tone. Try rubbing with Sugar Soap solution* which will remove polish and a large part of the stain. If this is not effective, use bleach*, following the manufacturer's directions.

Cigarette Burns

Don't despair if anyone lays burning cigarettes on the edge of a painted mantlepiece or dressing-table top to leave a dirty hollow. Scrape out the charred wood with a sharp penknife and fill proud with a cellulose filler* mixed with water or with a little of the paint you are using. Sand level when dry, continuing the sanding over the remainder of the surface to reduce gloss. Wash off, wipe over with tack rag and apply a thin finishing coat over the lot.

If you want an extra fine finish on a surface that is closely seen by visitors, make sure the brush is scrupulously clean, strain the paint and brush it on late at night when heavy outside traffic has ceased and everyone is in bed. Then the house will not tremble and dislodge otherwise inaccessible dust.

Natural Wood Finish*

Before deciding what form of *natural* finish to use on a completely stripped piece of furniture, see what manufacturers have to offer. Many of their products seal and provide a surface in the one operation, thus saving time. Some of them require no subsequent waxing.

Limed Oak

One way of freshening up limed oak is to pour a little ordinary metal polish into a saucer and leave for a day to allow some of the liquid to evaporate and form a stronger solution. Rub this on gently and the white of the polish will enter the grain, reviving the white streaky effect.

Dents and Chips

Bruised wood can often be brought level by dripping boiling water into the hollow and releasing the grain with a stout pin, or by applying a damp cloth and warm iron. The idea is to dampen the fibres and cause them to expand and fill the gaps. When this is not practicable, fill the dent with melted wax crayon or beeswax coloured with a powder pigment – sienna for reddish wood such as cedar, umber for brown woods such as oak – or use shoe polish or furniture polish.

Apply this filling with a hot soldering iron so that it drops into the right place, proud of the surface. When hard, pare level with a sharp knife.

Freshening Up Polished Furniture

Providing scratches that show light on dark-polished wood are not too deep, you can obliterate them by removing the polish from the affected parts with methylated spirit, painting scratch-cover polish* into the scratches with a fine brush, waiting until it has soaked in and then rubbing the whole piece of furniture with scratch-cover polish.

This may sound rather like botching, but it is surprising how effective it is. An annual touch-up in this way at spring cleaning time does not take long and will keep your furniture in spick-and span condition.

Hot plate marks can often be put right by rubbing round the affected part with methylated spirit. If this is not effective, try turning the furniture up so that the surface to be treated is vertical, and ignite the spirit. The aim here is to spread the surrounding good varnish onto the bad part.

Furniture that has been french-polished should never be waxed. All it needs is a periodic rub over with a chamois leather. If it shows signs of blooming (cloudiness) use vinegar and water, a teaspoonful to a half litre (pint); but experiment on an out-of-the-way part first to see how you go, increasing the strength if necessary. Don't make the solution too strong.

Ink stains soak in like a furniture stain. Sometimes they can be removed by rubbing with fine wirewool. Titivating the rubbed part to match the remainder will be difficult and it is often better to remove the whole of the finish on a marred member and completely refinish it. When using wirewool be sure you do not leave particles embedded in the wood where they will rust.

Dyeing Wood

Suppose, after stripping an existing varnish finish, you wish the underlying stained wood to be in a different colour – say a pastel shade – without obscuring the grain. Apply a bleach* to the wood, then a dye and varnish over it again. As more dye will sink into some parts, the effect will be something like limed oak in reverse, though the colour may be pink, light blue or yellow.

Or, with an open-grain wood, you can use an emulsion or oil-bound water paint, allowing the paint to soak into the grain and scraping off surplus while it is still wet. Then varnish.

Experiment with these two methods on a piece of wood of the same texture as that of the surface you are treating.

Picture Frames

Straight coloured picture frames that have become chipped at the corners can often be put right with a cellulose filler* and touched in with paint of the same colour so that the repair is hardly noticed. When entirely repainting, remove the glass and use an aerosol paint* to get a smooth finish. Pass the spray fairly quickly along the grooved parts first, as the paint will have farther to travel and will tend to fan out and become thin. When dry, spray the whole frame normally.

Ornamental gold frames often have the valleys in a deeper or lighter colour than the relief parts. This can be achieved by painting the whole frame in a scumble*, using the second colour required. When hard, dry-brush over the relief parts with gold paint*, as is described on page 128, and varnish all over.

Few ordinary paint-shops stock scumble, as it is normally used for wood graining which is not at present in fashion. You may have to go to a builders' merchant.

Use a finely pigmented gold paint. Cheap materials contain relatively large metallic particles which rise to the surface of the film and become tarnished.

To get a *really* smooth finish, brush varnish over the relief parts and when it becomes sticky, rub in fine bronze powder with a polishing motion. If done carefully this looks almost as good as gold leaf.

Brass and Copper

To preserve the brilliance of brass ornaments, clean thoroughly with metal polish. Then scrub in hot soda water to dissolve remnants of polish, and immerse in clean hot water to remove the soda. Dry thoroughly and immediately coat with clear cellulose*. This does not give quite the brilliance of newly polished metal but it saves an enormous amount of work.

As cellulose is critical of even the slightest suspicion of grease, try not to handle the articles before painting.

Copper feed pipes to a radiator cannot very well be immersed, so clean them with white spirit and fine wirewool followed by soda water, followed by clear hot water. Then cellulose them without undue handling. See footnote on page 4 regarding *white spirit.*

Pipes may be painted with a colour, after cleaning, by using two finishing coats of an alkyd resin paint*. Don't use under-coating which is too highly pigmented to adhere properly; and touch in with aluminium primer sealer only over joints at which a green stain may bleed through.

17
First Aid for Fences

Has your fence a dangerous list? Does it wobble in a high wind?

If so, the cause of the trouble is below ground level where moisture from the surrounding subsoil has rotted the posts, causing a furriness on the outside. However firmly the surrounding soil is tamped down it will never provide the grip it did when the fence was new.

Here is one way of making good the damage – one that you will no doubt agree is neater and cheaper than the use of concrete spurs.

Trowel out the surrounding soil to expose the stump. Scrape away furry wood and remove as many of the scrapings as you can; they will contain rot-producing fungi. Work in dry weather, after a prolonged period of drought. This is not absolutely necessary, but working on wood that is not sodden will help.

Now place a few stones in the bottom of the hole to serve as drainage and tamp them well down.

From your local foundry or ironmonger order strips of mild steel about 40 mm. wide and 6 mm. thick ($1\frac{1}{2}$ in. × $\frac{1}{4}$ in.). For a shoulder-high fence the strips should be a metre (3 ft.) long. A higher fence will need strips longer in proportion, and for anything higher than 2·5 metres (8 ft) they should be wider and thicker as well. Get two strips for each post, and ask the supplier to bore two holes in each 10 mm. ($\frac{3}{8}$ in.) in diameter and 250 mm. (10 in.) apart, the top one being 50 mm. (2 in.) from one end.

Clean off foundry deposits by scraping and rubbing with emery cloth and coat with zinc chromate primer, followed by one undercoat and two finishing coats of an alkyd resin paint* of a colour to match the upper reaches of the fence. Where appearance is not of first importance, two coats of bituminous paint – which is cheaper – can be used over the zinc chromate primer. If it is impossible to remove all rust patches apply a rust solvent* or phosphating material.

The job will not take so long as it sounds because strips for every post can be treated at the same time and, in any case, it is a once-only operation and is worth the extra trouble.

Stand two strips in the hole you have made, one on each side of the post on which you are working, screw holes uppermost, and attach to the post with galvanised coach screws of size to fit the holes. Coach screws ($2\frac{1}{2}$ in.) are recommended because you can tighten them with a spanner. To ease entry of the screws bore holes in the post first, slightly less in length and diameter than the bolts, and smear the threads with Vaseline or old engine oil. Insert a washer under the head of each screw.

Place a plumb-bob or spirit level against one side of the post to make sure it is upright, and prop it temporarily in that position.

Fill the hole with mortar comprising one part by volume of cement and three parts of sharp sand, with sufficient water to make a puddingy mix. Intersperse stones or broken pieces of brick between each shovelful – so economising in mortar. Don't use concrete (which is mortar with shingle added), because in the process of shovelling the aggregate could shift the post from its upright position.

Bring the mortar to just above ground level and trowel the mortar surface away from the post so that rain will run off.

Fig. 33 shows the principle.

Touch in exposed bolt heads with paint and replace the soil before removing the props.

Work on one post at a time, and the remaining posts will support the fence. Leave at least a day before starting on the next post, to allow the first lot of mortar to harden.

That takes care of underground sources of trouble. But weather will no doubt have affected the tops of the posts, causing incipient decay (page 86) to show in the end grain of the wood.

Scrape off furriness and cover the tops with sheet zinc; or small pieces of bituminous felt may be used, which is cheaper. Use wire nails for zinc and large headed clout nails for felt – the non-ferrous variety so that you will not be troubled with rust.

Sometimes arris rails break. Renew them before the posts are fixed, otherwise you will have to 'spring' them into the

Fig. 33. Close-boarded fence with arris rails, gravel board and post in need of repair.

mortises. Secure the tenon ends into the mortises by boring holes and knocking in pieces of dowelling. Arris rails that are sagging can be prevented from getting worse by placing a supporting block of wood, partly buried in the ground, under the middle of the bottom one. If an arris rail is loose but otherwise sound, tighten it by driving oak wedges into the mortise, nailing them in position.

As an alternative, you can buy non-ferrous metal brackets to secure the arris rails. By using these, the rails can be renewed after you have finished work on the posts.

Wooden fences need creosoting about every two years, which is a nuisance because the operation will injure adjacent plantlife. Indeed, creosote is a very effective weed-killer and will put an end to all vegetation on to which it splashes.

If you do not intend digging the bed, separating roots and replanting round about the same period as you are creosoting, bend existing foliage down away from the fence, keeping it in that position with odd pieces of timber, and cover with sheeting.

Proprietary wood preservatives* last as long as five years, and you may consider their extra cost over that of creosote well justified.

Before applying creosote or other preservative to a neglected fence, wirebrush off moss and loose dirt to allow the liquid to soak into the pores and cellular structure of the timber. If moss is particularly obstinate in crevices which cannot easily be reached, heat the fence by scattering the flame of a blow-lamp — but don't concentrate on one part for too long or you will be faced with a conflagration! The flame will also warm up the surface, making it easier for the preservative to enter the wood. The blow-lamp can be used by a companion working in front of you.

A simpler method of treating old fence posts that are not too far gone — that is to say, they are still firm but it will not be long before they start to wobble — is to bore a hole, about 10 mm. ($\frac{3}{8}$ in.) in diameter, slanting down at an angle of 45 degrees, at a little above ground level. Through a funnel pour in creosote. Allow it to soak in and fill again. Then stop up the mouth of the hole with mastic compound or putty to prevent rain from entering. The idea is indicated where the foot of the post is shown in Fig. 33. Creosote within the hole will be drawn up and down with the grain of the wood, killing internal fungus growths as it goes.

A word of warning!
Make sure that the fence is your responsibility. You won't want to put a lot of work into a job that your neighbour should be doing. If the arris rails are on your side, then in all probability the fence is yours – unless somebody in the past has done the nailing on the wrong side. There is nothing in law to say that arris rails must be on your side; it is just custom – perhaps a compliment to your neighbour in presenting him with the best side of the fence.

As a general rule, a householder is responsible for the boundary on one side of his garden and at the foot. If you are in doubt, consult the deeds of your house.

Appendix 1
Decorating Materials

Choice of decorating materials is very much a personal one, and the following chart is intended only as a guide to help in the final selection. It is drawn up on a balance between three factors – appearance, durability and cost.

All surfaces intended to be decorated must be clean, dry and firm.

Materials for Various Surfaces

Interiors	*Surface*	*First choice*	*Second choice*	*Third choice*
Living rooms and bedrooms	Walls	Paper or vinyl	Emulsion paint	Water paint
	Ceilings	Emulsion paint	Paper	Water paint
	Woodwork	Gloss paint	Eggshell paint	Flat paint
Hall and stairway	Walls	Emulsion paint	Paper or vinyl	Water paint
	Ceilings	Emulsion paint	Water paint	Paper
	Woodwork	Eggshell paint	Gloss paint	Flat paint
Kitchen and bathroom where anticondensation paint may not be needed	Walls	Gloss paint	Vinyl or washable wallpaper	Eggshell paint
	Ceilings	Emulsion paint	Eggshell paint	Gloss paint
	Woodwork	Gloss paint	Eggshell paint	—
	Furniture	Polyurethane paint	Gloss paint	—

Exteriors	*Surface*	*First choice*	*Second choice*	*Third choice*
Walls	Brick	Leave them as they are	Brick dye	Brick paint
	Cement rendering	Masonry paint	Emulsion paint	Cement paint
	Stucco	Oleoresinous paint	Limewash	Emulsion paint
	Timber-faced	UV absorbent varnish	Madison sealer	Gloss paint
Woodwork	Doors, windows, etc.	Gloss paint	—	—
	Fences	Proprietary wood preservative	Creosote	Gloss paint

Exteriors	Surface	First choice	Second choice	Third choice
Gutters, pipes and sheds	Outside of iron gutters, downpipes, etc.	Gloss paint	Bituminous paint	—
	Inside of iron gutters	Bituminous paint	Gloss paint	—
	Outside of asbestos gutters; also asbestos sheds	Emulsion paint	Bituminous paint	—
	Inside of asbestos gutters	Bituminous paint	Epoxy resin paint	—
	Vinyl gutters and downpipes	Don't paint	—	—

Here are some points to note about the paints mentioned above. See Products Index for manufacturers.

Bituminous paint. Extremely waterproof. Soon loses its gloss and tends to craze under a hot sun.

Brick dye. Will last about two years. Some brands have waterproofing properties.

Brick paint. Mostly applied direct to the bricks. May aggravate interstitial condensation (see page 84).

Cement paint. Mixture of cement and water with other additives.

Creosote. Cheap, but will not last for long.

Emulsion paint. Reasonable in price and easily applied. Use a copolymer outdoor grade.

Epoxy resin paint. In two packs to be mixed immediately before use. Difficult to obtain in small quantities.

Gloss, eggshell and flat paints. For all wood, ironwork and most other building surfaces. Use the alkyd resin types – gloss outside; gloss, eggshell or flat inside.

Limewash. Sprinkle one part by weight of tallow in small lumps over 20 parts of quicklime. Slake with just sufficient water to form a thick paste, stirring all the time. Leave to cool and thin with water to the required consistency. If you have difficulty in getting tallow, use linseed or castor oil. Lime-resisting pigments only should be used for adding colour to the mix, and they should be added to the water before the lime is slaked. Very little blue will make a brilliant white. Apply with a grass brush or one made of nylon filaments – not a bristle brush.

Madison sealer. For all good woods, particularly cedar. Composed mainly of oil, wax and white spirit. Enhances the grain and leaves a pleasing low gloss. Tends to collect surface dirt.

Masonry paint. The newer masonry paints are a vast improvement on older types. When applied over a wall that has been adequately prepared, the more expensive will last ten years.

Oleoresinous paint. An old-fashioned oil paint made from natural resins. Used widely before the advent of alkyd resin paints and not so critical of a doubtful surface.

Polyurethane paint. Originally in two packs which had to be mixed before use. May now be obtained in modified form in one pack. Sets so hard that, when it chips, sanding for subsequent repainting is sometimes difficult. Some tend to peel when used outside.

UV absorbent varnish. A varnish specially formulated to resist disruption by the sun's ultra-violet rays. Expensive; but should last five years in exposed positions. Not suitable for metal surfaces.

Vinyl wallcovering. Will last almost a lifetime. Easily washed.

Water paint. Not so durable as emulsion, but may be preferred because of colour range. Water paint is sometimes called oil-bound washable distemper – not to be confused with true distemper which is size-bound and easily rubbed off.

Wood Preservative. Its cost above that of creosote will be more than repaid by longer life.

Primers

A multi-coat oil-paint system comprises primer, undercoat and one or two finishing coats. The function of a primer is to seal pores in the surface or to inhibit the spread of corrosion, and to form an anchor for succeeding coats. That of the undercoat is to fill minor irregularities in the surface and to hide whatever colour is underneath (some colours of finishing coats do the latter equally as well). Finishing coats provide colour and good appearance and withstand attacks by the weather.

The welt and uppers of a shoe will stand many resolings. The same applies to a primer. Provided it is firmly adhering it will outlast several undercoats and finishing coats of a material similar to that previously applied. Being the foundation, the primer is the most important part of a paint system, and it is essential to use the correct one, in the first place, for each type of building surface, as follows.

Building surface	Type	Primer
Timber	Structural softwoods	Wood primer
	Porous hardwoods	Wood primer thinned with about 15 per cent white spirit, followed when dry with unthinned wood primer
	Highly resinous woods	Aluminium primer-sealer
	Teak and other 'greasy' woods	Teak sealer
Building boards	Plasterboard	Alkali-resisting primer
	Standard hardboard	Hardboard primer, plaster primer or emulsion paint thinned with an equal quantity of water
	Tempered hardboard	Thinned emulsion paint
	Fire-resistant board	Alkali-resisting primer
	Asbestos sheeting	Alkali-resisting primer
	Heat-resisting asbestos	Thinned emulsion paint
Plaster	Old	Plaster primer
	New	Alkali-resisting primer
	Powdery	Penetrating primer
Metal	Iron and steel	Zinc chromate, red lead, zinc-rich or calcium plumbate primer
	New zinc and new galvanised iron (which has a bright silvery colour)	Calcium plumbate primer
	Weathered zinc and weathered galvanised iron (which has a dull grey colour)	Zinc chromate or calcium plumbate primer
	Aluminium	Zinc chromate primer
	Brass and lead	No primer
	Copper	Aluminium primer only in parts where a green stain may show through. Otherwise, no primer

Some primers and finishing coats have undercoating properties – which means that, when used inside a house, the number of coats of paint can be decreased. Sometimes erroneously called one-coat paints, those that include undercoat and finishing properties may be thicker than normal coats, yet are not sufficiently thick to provide the necessary protection for outside work, unless more than one coat is applied.

Emulsion paint. On most surfaces the primer to use under an emulsion paint finish, is emulsion thinned with an equal quantity of water; but on friable surfaces use a penetrating primer.

Epoxy resin paint. Follow manufacturer's directions regarding primer.

Masonry and cement paints. Follow the manufacturer's directions regarding primer.

Wallpaper. Seal the surface with well-thinned glue size.

Painting Over Previously Painted Surfaces

Although it is advisable, when repainting, to use the same type of paint as that previously applied, in cases noted below you can completely change the system. Sometimes the table below has an unequivocal yes or no. But decorating is like gardening, full of ifs and buts, and so other entries give numbers which refer to full explanations following.

For instance, oil paint will take over old emulsion that is clean, firm and dry, and therefore 'Yes' appears for this combination. It will also take over previously applied oil paint that has been sanded down, and so here reference to note 1 is indicated. Emulsion will take over oil paint that has been sanded – but only in normal living rooms, not in steamy atmospheres (notes 1 and 2). Oil paint will show 'bleed' stains if applied over old bitumen (7), but emulsion will not, though it is likely to crack or craze (8).

Existing Decoration	Oil paint	Emulsion	Size-bound distemper	Water paint	Bituminous paint	Cellulose paint	Polyurethane paint	Wallpaper
					New decoration			
Oil paint	1	1,2	1, 2	1, 2	1	3	3	1, 4
Emulsion	Yes	Yes	Yes	Yes	Yes	3	3	Yes
Size-bound distemper			*Will take no new decoration: 5*					
Water paint	Yes	Yes	Yes	Yes	Yes	3	3	6
Bituminous paint	7	8	Yes	8	Yes	3, 8	3, 8	No
Cellulose paint	1	1, 2	1, 2	1, 2	1	3	3	1, 4
Polyurethane paint	1	1, 2	1, 2	1, 2	1	3	3	1, 4
Wallpaper	9	10	10	10	No	No	No	11

1. Yes! provided the existing gloss is reduced with fine waterproof abrasive paper, used wet. Where the substrate is wood, sand only in the direction of the grain – to avoid scratch marks.

2. Not, however, in steamy kitchens and bathrooms where moisture will penetrate the new paint (which, being water-borne, is porous), condense against a hard, cold surface and push the new coating off.

3. There is a danger of the solvents in the new coating activating the old and causing it to 'lift'. This does not apply to the latest one-can polyurethanes applied to previous coatings which, through age, have become extremely hard. Consult the paint manufacturer's literature when in doubt.

4. Use a paste containing a fungicide and, to provide extra 'tooth', mix a handful of sifted whiting or fine pumice powder in a bowl of paste. Paste has a constricting action and this may damage paint adhesion.

5. Size-bound (non-washable) distemper is too powdery and loosely bound to permit further coating with any type of paint. Before redecorating, strip the old material completely with warm water to which a little ammonia has been added.

6. Yes! provided the wall has been sized.

7. The solvents in the oil paint will activate the bitumen and cause 'bleeding', unless the bitumen is first sealed with two coats of aluminium primer sealer. If the bitumen is fairly new you may have to apply a coat of shellac followed by a coat of aluminium primer sealer. The shellac has the greater sealing power but it does not make such a sound base for subsequent coats of paint as does aluminium primer sealer. There are also very good proprietary sealers on the market.

8. Applying a hard new coating over a relatively soft bitumen may cause 'crazing' (fine hair cracks).

9. Not advised. The oil of the paint causes the fibres of the paper to become brittle.

10. Yes – over plain and light patterned papers. No – over papers printed in metallic inks (gold or silver), deep reds and some turquoises, where there is a danger of the pattern 'bleeding' through the new coating.

11. New wallpaper paste soaking through old paper will activate the original paste which may be nearing the end of its functional life – resulting in the whole lot parting company from the wall. This does not happen when lining paper is being hung under a wallpaper because the paste is new.

Appendix 2
Specifications for the Treatment of Rot in Wood

The following specifications, reproduced from *The Dry Rot Problem* by Dr Norman E. Hickin (Hutchinson) by kind permission of the author, are used by timber infestation surveyors employed by Rentokil Laboratories as a basis for inspection and method of working.

Full Dry-Rot Treatment

1. Cut out all timbers showing transverse or cuboidal cracking, brown coloration, presence of white mycelium, etc., and all apparently sound timber within a radius of one metre of the nearest visibly decayed timber. Carefully remove all such decayed timber from the premises by the shortest practicable route and burn.

2. Hack away all plaster and rendering coats and remove any skirtings, linings, studdings, panelling and ceilings necessary to trace the fullest extent of mycelium, etc., over or through adjacent brick, block, concrete or timber surfaces.

3. Thoroughly clean with a wire brush all such surfaces as walling, partitions, sleeper walls, surface concrete and also all adjoining timber, and any steel and pipe work within the area up to a radius of 1·5 metres from the farthest extent of suspected infection. Carefully remove from the premises by the shortest practical route all dust and debris existing and ensuing from the operation and burn.

4. Subject to heat-treatment all brick, block, concrete and earth surfaces with a heat machine, until too hot to touch, to kill surface mycelium and hyphae and to dry out excessive moisture.

5. Apply fungicidal fluid to all such brick, block, concrete and earth surfaces at the specified rate.

6. Apply two liberal coats of fungicidal fluid to all timber surfaces adjacent to cutting away, to a distance of 1·5 metres from cutting away, allowing the first coat to be absorbed before applying the second coat.

7. Select thoroughly dry, well-seasoned timber for replacement; cut to size; give two liberal brush coats of fungicidal fluid to all surfaces. Stand ends of timber in a pail of the fluid for a few minutes before placing and fixing.

8. Re-render in cement, lime and sand (1 : 1 : 6) all previously rendered surfaces, including any necessary dubbing out. Then apply a floating coat of zinc oxychloride (z.o.c.) plaster over the rendering coat (where a setting coat of wall plaster is subsequently to be applied) to an area extending 300 mm. (12 in.) beyond any previously attacked timber (or up to 600 mm. or 24 in. maximum in extremely severe cases). Render all adjacent surfaces around z.o.c. with a second coat of cement, lime and sand to receive setting coat of retarded hemi-hydrate plaster (board finish) and leave set ready for decorating by the client.

9. Alternatively, for areas not to be replastered, apply two coats of z.o.c. paint in lieu of z.o.c. plaster. Renew any ceilings or soffits taken down in course of eradication works in plasterboard and scrim and set in retarded hemi-hydrate plaster (board finish) and leave ready for decorating by the client.

10. Cut away for, provide and fix and make good to air bricks or make alternative arrangements necessary to provide adequately increased ventilation. Remove any defective damp courses from sleeper walls and provide and lay new lead-lined bitumen d.p.c. or carry out alternative arrangements to prevent rising damp before fixing any pre-treated replacement joists.

Full Wet-Rot Treatment

Provided that the cause of damp can be removed and the timber allowed to dry out, no further attack will develop in timbers not already attacked. The following treatment deals with:

(*a*) The renewal of timber which has already suffered breakdown.

(*b*) The protection of timbers already attacked but still retaining adequate structural strength.

(*c*) The protection of adjacent timbers in which attack may be latent.

1. Timbers in the area of fungal attack are to be tested with a strong-pointed instrument to determine the extent of sub-surface breakdown, and all timber that has suffered surface or sub-surface breakdown due to fungal attack is to be cut out and removed from premises and burnt, together with all dust, dirt and debris existing in the area of attack, or ensuing from cutting-away operations.

2. Select thoroughly dry well-seasoned timber for replacement, cut to size, and give two liberal brush coats of fungicidal fluid over all surfaces of those replacement timbers and of adjacent surfaces of existing timbers and brick, block and concrete areas before placing the replacement timbers in position and fixing.

3. Remove any defective damp courses from sleeper walls and provide and lay new lead-lined bitumen d.p.c. before fixing pre-treated replacement timbers.

4. Re-render in cement, lime and sand (1 : 1 : 6) and float and set in anhydrous (wall finish) plaster any wall surfaces in the area of attack. Renew in gypsum plasterboard, and scrim and set in retarded hemi-hydrate plaster (board finish) any ceiling surfaces removed in the course of the timber treatment and leave ready for decorating by the client.

Appendix 3
Metrication

Decimalisation, introduced in 1971, was compulsory. Metrication is voluntary – which rather complicates matters in as far as timetables, drawn up by industries usually through trade federations, are not binding on manufacturers. Most products are now sold metric.

Nearly all standard metric sizes of building materials are close to imperial standards, though slightly smaller. For example, standard lengths of timber increase in steps of 300 mm., which is just under a foot. A piece of 50 × 25 mm. is just under the old 2 × 1 in.

For all practical purposes, the metric sizes of hardboard, plywood, particle board, glass and other sheet materials are no different from those you are accustomed to. The diameters of plastic piping, manufactured in metre lengths, remain unchanged, although described in millimetres. Paint is sold in containers holding 100 millilitres (near $\frac{1}{5}$ pint) to 25 litres ($5\frac{1}{2}$ gallons).

As the construction industry prefers multiples and submultiples in thousands, metric measurements given in this book are confined to millimetres and metres (the former being one-thousandth part of the latter). This does not mean that the centimetre is an inconvenient size; it often appears in manufacturers' instructional literature.

Purely for reference purposes and *not* for the ordering of materials, here is a list of *actual* conversions to two or three places of decimals:

Length

1 inch = 25·4 millimetres (mm.)   1 mm. = 0·039 inch

1 foot = 0·305 metres (m.)   1 m. = 3·281 feet
    or 1·094 yards

1 yard = 0·914 metres (m.)

Capacity

1 pint = 0·568 litres   1 litre = 1·76 pints,
(The abbreviation of   0·88 quarts or
litres as l. is not   0·22 gallons
advised as it might be
mistaken for the
figure one)

1 quart = 1·137 litres

1 gallon = 4·546 litres

Weight

1 ounce = 28·35 grammes (g.)   1 g. = 0·035 ounce

1 pound = 453·6 g. or   1 kg. = 2·205 pounds
0·454 kilograms (kg.)

1 hundredweight = 50·8 kg.

1 ton = 1016 kg.

Products Index

This Index is provided for the convenience of readers who are undecided on what product to buy. It gives the addresses of manufacturers in case difficulty is experienced in finding a local stockist, and will also come in useful for getting instructional literature.

The Index is by no means complete and comprises only those products that have been used by the writer with satisfaction. There will be similar products on the market, perhaps equally as good.

Asterisks (*) in the foregoing text denote where references in this Index may be found. To trace them, use the operative phrase; for instance –

Alkyd resin paint comes under A – Alkyd resin paint.
Proprietary sealer comes under S – Sealer for bituminous, creosoted and stained surfaces.

Where a generic name appears in close proximity to another mention of the same name, only the first mention bears an asterisk and only one mention is in the Index. Manufacturers' addresses were checked at the time of going to press.

Product	Page	Brand name	Manufacturer
Aerosol paint	128, 129, 133	**Humbrol**	Humbrol Ltd, Marfleet, Hull HU9 5NE
Alkyd resin paint	4, 12, 57, 60, 63, 128, 134, 136, 141	**Dulux gloss and eggshell**	ICI Paints Division, Slough, Bucks SL2 5DS
		Permoglaze	Blundell-Permoglaze Ltd, 37 Queen Sq, London WC1
		Brolac	Berger Paints, Freshwater Rd, Dagenham, Essex RM8 1RV

Product	Page	Brand name	Manufacturer
Anti-rust compound	5	**See Rust solvents**	
Anti-condensation paint	60, 75	**Anticon**	Silexine Paints Ltd, Abbey Rd, Barking, Essex
Asbestos-filler	125	**Rawlplastic**	The Rawlplug Co. Ltd, 147 London Rd, Kingston-upon-Thames, Surrey KT2 6NR
		Screwfix	Expandite Ltd, Western Rd, Bracknell, Berks RG12 1RH
Bath enamel	63	**Joy**	Turnbridges Ltd, 72 Longley Rd, London SW17
Bath	63	—	Allied Ironfounders Ltd, Cadby Rd, Sunbury on-Thames, Middx
Bath re-enamelled in situ	63	—	Renubath Ltd, 596 Chiswick High Rd, London W4 5RS
Bath stain remover	62	**Jenolite Bath Stain Remover**	Jenolite Ltd, 13–17 Rathbone St, London W1
		R. B. 70	Renubath Ltd, 596 Chiswick High Rd, London W4 5RS
Bleach for wood	130, 132	**Rustin's Wood Bleach**	Rustins Ltd, Waterloo Rd, Cricklewood, London NW2 7TX
Bonding agent for mortar	80	**Bondcrete**	B.C. Products Ltd, 29 Eve Rd, Woking, Surrey
		Dufix	Plant Protection Ltd, Fernhurst, Haslemere, Surrey
Brick dye	3, 140, 141	**Bricktone**	Bertram Bennett Ltd, Bullock St, Birmingham 7
Brick paint	140, 141	**Rustin's Brick and Tile Paint**	Rustins Ltd, Waterloo Rd, Cricklewood, London NW2 7TX
Castors	26	**Clayrite**	Howard Clayton-Wright Ltd, Wellesbourne, Warks

Product	Page	Brand name	Manufacturer
Castors	26	**Flexello**	Flexello Castors & Wheels Ltd, Bath Rd, Slough, Bucks SL1 4ED
Cavity insulating membrane	83	**Ufoam**	Four Seasons Window Co. Ltd, Havelock Rd, Southall, Middx
		Ufoam	ICI Insulation Service Ltd, PO Box 100, Welwyn Garden City, Herts
Cellulose filler	25, 32, 93, 128, 130, 132	**Interior Polyfilla**	Polycell Products Ltd, Broadwater Rd, Welwyn Garden City, Herts
Cellulose paint	144	**Brushing Belco**	ICI Paints Division, Slough, Bucks SL2 5DS
Cement paint	10, 140, 141	**Paintcrete**	George Lillington & Co. Ltd, Willow Lane, Mitcham, Surrey CR4 4UR
		Snowcem	The Cement Marketing Co. Ltd (Blue Circle Group), Portland House, Stag Place, London SW1E 5BJ
Ceramic tiles	63	**Cristal**	H & R Johnson Ltd, PO Box 1, Turnstall, Stoke-on-Trent, Staffs
Clear cellulose	133	**Clear Brushing Belco**	ICI Paints Division, Slough, Bucks SL2 5DS
Contact adhesive	65	**Evo-Stik Impact**	Evode Ltd, Stafford
Electro-osmotic process	82	—	Rentokil Laboratories Ltd, School Lane, Fetcham, Leather-head, Surrey
Emulsion paint	6, 11, 13, 60, 140, 141, 143, 144	**Dulux emulsion and Supercover**	ICI Paints Division, Slough, Bucks SL2 5DS
		Pammastic	Blundell-Permoglaze Ltd, 37 Queen Sq, London WC1
Epoxy resin ad-hesive	10	**Araldite**	CIBA-GEIGY (UK) Ltd, Plastics Divi-sion, Duxford, Cambridge CB2 4QA

Product	Page	Brand name	Manufacturer
Epoxy resin adhesive	10	**Twinbond**	Holt Products Ltd, Vulcan Way, New Addington, Surrey
Fireclay	38	**Pyruma**	Purimachos Ltd, 14 Waterloo Rd, Bristol
		Tiluma	J. H. Sankey & Son Ltd, Ilford, Essex
Fire retardant emulsion	34	**Timonox**	Associated Lead Manufacturers Ltd, PO Box 247, Clements House, 14 Gresham St, London EC2P 2JS
Fungicidal fluid for rot in wood	86, 88	**Cuprinol**	The Cuprinol Preservation Centre, Stag Place, London SW1E 5AP
		Rentokil	Rentokil Laboratories Ltd, School Lane, Fetcham, Leatherhead, Surrey
		Universal Solignum Preservative	Solignum Ltd, Thames Rd, Crayford, Dartford, Kent DA1 4QJ
Gold paint	133	**Ardenbrite**	Thos Pavitt & Sons Ltd, 57 Farringdon Rd, London EC1
Hard stopping	14, 55, 127	**Brummer Green Label (outdoor grade, waterproof). Yellow Label for interior use**	Clam-Brummer Ltd, Maxwell Rd, Boreham Wood, Herts
		Plastic Wood	The Rawlplug Co. Ltd, 147 Kingston Rd, Kingston-upon-Thames, Surrey KT2 6NR
		Exterior Polyfilla	Polycell Holdings Ltd, Broadwater Rd, Welwyn Garden City, Herts

Product	Page	Brand name	Manufacturer
Heat-resisting asbestos	39, 46	**Asbestolux**	Cape Building Products Ltd, Cowley Bridge Works, Uxbridge, Middx
Insulating material	77	**Rocksil**	Cape Insulation Ltd, Stirling, Scotland FK7 7RW
Laminated plastic sheeting	65	**Formica and Formica Beautyboard**	Formica Ltd, 84–86 Regent St, London W1A 1DL
Louvre windows	47, 53, 74	—	Louvre Centre, 61–65 Judd St, London WC1
		—	Glassworks (Greenford) Ltd, 413 Greenford Rd, Greenford, Middx
		Louvre King	International Window Co. Ltd, Braintree Rd, South Ruislip, Middx HA4 0XW
Masonry paint	10, 140, 142	**Sandtex Matt**	The Cement Marketing Co. Ltd (Blue Circle Group), Portland House, Stag Place, London SW1E 5BJ
		Silexine Stone Paint	Silexine Paints Ltd, Abbey Rd, Barking, Essex
		Weathershield	ICI Paints Division, Slough, Bucks SL2 5DX
Masonry paint for doubtful sur-faces	12	**Rogstone**	Dixon's Paints Ltd, Ajax Works, Hertford Rd, Barking, Essex
		Xterno Stucco Paint	Leyland Paints Ltd, Northgate, Leyland, Lancs
Mastic compound	13, 79	**Seelastik**	Expandite Ltd, Chase Rd, London NW10
Mixic acid	14	—	Wright & Sumner Ltd, 8 Johnson St, London E1
Mould inhibitor	19	**ICI Mould Inhibitor**	ICI Paints Division, Slough, Bucks SL2 5DX

Product	*Page*	*Brand name*	*Manufacturer*
Mould inhibitor	19	**Santobrite**	Monsanto Chemicals Ltd, 10–18 Victoria St, London SW1; and Victoria Way, Burgess Hill, Sussex
Natural wood finish	130	**Colron and Ronseal**	Ronuk Ltd, Portslade, Sussex
		Luroc	Alexander, Fergusson & Co. Ltd, 50 Ruchill St, Glasgow NW
		Rustin's Wood Finishes	Rustins Ltd, Waterloo Rd, London NW2 7TX
		Speedeneez	Thos Pavitt & Sons Ltd, 57 Farringdon Rd, London EC1
		Translac	A. Sanderson & Co. Ltd, Kingston Paint Works, Ropery St, Hull HU3 2BX
Non-washable size bound distemper	40, 144	**Ceilingite**	T & W Farmiloe Ltd, Horsenden Lane South, Perivale, Greenford, Middx
One coat paint	143	**Dulux Super 3**	ICI Paints Division, Slough, Bucks SL2 5DS
		Magicote	Berger Paints, Freshwater Rd, Dagenham, Essex RM8 1RU
Paint remover (or stripper)	14, 48, 129	**Nitromors**	Wilcot (Parent) Co. Ltd, Alexandra Park, Fishponds, Bristol BS16 2BQ
		Strypit	Rustins Ltd, Waterloo Rd, Cricklewood, London NW2 7TX
Plastic metal stopping	5, 57, 58, 111	**Isopon**	W. David & Sons Ltd, 47–49 Caledonian Rd, London N1
		Plasting Padding (hard and elastic grades)	Plastic Padding Ltd, Sands Industrial Estate, High Wycombe, Bucks

Product	Page	Brand name	Manufacturer
Plastic wood	127	**Rawlplug Plastic Wood**	The Rawlplug Co. Ltd, 147 London Rd, Kingston-upon-Thames, Surrey KT2 6NR
		Rustin's Plastic Wood	Rustins Ltd, Waterloo Rd, London NW2 7TX
Poly-ethylene wall covering	17	**Novelle**	ICI Paints Division, Slough, Bucks SL2 5DS. *Refer to local ICI sales office for list of stockists*
Polyurethane paint	65, 128, 140, 142, 144, 145	**Kingston Diamond**	A. Sanderson & Co. Ltd, Kingston Paint Works Ropery St, Hull HU3 2BX
		Permoglaze Polyurethane	Blundell-Permoglaze Ltd, 37 Queen Sq, London WC1
PVA adhesive	10	**Dufix**	Plant Protection Ltd, Fernhurst, Haslemere, Surrey
Roof paint	3	**Rustin's Brick and Tile Paint**	Rustins Ltd, Waterloo Rd, Cricklewood, London NW2 7TX
Rust solvents, stabilisers and removers	54, 65, 123, 136	**Galvafroid**	Expandite Ltd, Chase Rd, London NW10
		Kurust	A. Sanderson & Co. Ltd, Kingston Paint Works, Ropery St, Hull HU3 2BX
		Jenolite Rust Remover	Jenolite Ltd, 13–17 Rathbone St, London W1
		Rusta Resta	Blundell-Permoglaze Ltd, 37 Queen Sq, London WC1
Scratch cover polish	131	**Joy**	Turnbridges Ltd, 72 Longley Rd, London SW17
Scumble	133	—	J. H. Ratcliffe, 135a Linaker St, Southport, Lancs

Product	Page	Brand name	Manufacturer
Scuttle for rollering paint at a height	12	**LAD-A-LOK**	Leng-Armac Ltd, Stirling Corner, Barnet By-pass, Boreham Wood, Herts
Sealer for bituminous, creosoted and stained surfaces	15, 129, 145	**Bleed Seal**	International Decorative Paints, Henrietta House, London W1
Self-adhesive vinyl sheeting	44, 64	**Con-Tact**	Storey Bros & Co. Ltd, White Cross, Lancaster
		Fablon	Commercial Plastics Ltd, Berkeley Square House, Berkeley Sq, London W1
Skarsten scraper	57	**Skarsten**	Skarsten Manufacturing Co. Ltd, Welwyn Garden City, Herts
Sodium fluoride	87	—	*Your local chemist should order from manufacturers at your request*
Sugar soap	130	**Manger's Sugar Soap**	J. Manger & Sons Ltd, PO Box 117, Tredegar Rd, London E3
Supatap	112	**Supatap**	F. H. Bourner & Co. Ltd, Manor Royal, Crawley, Sussex
Tank and pipe lagging	110	**Rocksil**	Cape Insulation Ltd, Stirling, Scotland FK7 7RW
Ultra-violet ray absorbent varnish	12, 140, 142	**Timbercoat**	Blundell-Permoglaze Ltd, 37 Queen Sq, London WC1
Underfloor draught fire	36, 87	**Baxi**	Richard Baxendale & Sons Ltd, Chorley, Lancs
Vinyl wall covering	17, 60, 140, 142	**Vymura**	ICI Paints Division, Slough, Bucks SL2 5DS
Wall plugs	125	**Rawlplug**	The Rawlplug Co. Ltd, 147 London Rd, Kingston-upon-Thames, Surrey KT2 6NR

Product	*Page*	*Brand name*	*Manufacturer*
Wood preservative	56, 138, 140, 142	**Cuprinol**	The Cuprinol Preservation Centre, 5 Stag Place, London SW 1E 5AP
		Rentokil	Rentokil Laboratories Ltd, School Lane, Fetcham, Leatherhead, Surrey
		Solignum	Solignum Ltd, Thames Rd, Crayford, Dartford, Kent DA1 4QJ
Wood preservation experts	88, 94, 146–148	—	See *Wood preservative*
Woodworm fluid	90, 93, 99	**Rentokil**	Rentokil Laboratories Ltd, School Lane, Fetcham, Leatherhead, Surrey
Woven chair seats	127	—	Eaton Raffia Shop, 16 Manette St, London W1V 5LB
Zinc or magnesium silicofluoride	13	—	*Your local chemist should order from manufacturers at your request*

Index

Algae removal, 13
Arris rails, 137
Asbestos painting, 6, 13

Bath, care of, 62
Bathroom,
    condensation in, 62
    decoration of, 59–60
    heating in, 62, 100
Bleaching wood, 130
Brass, preserving brilliance of,
    133
Bricks,
    cutting, 10
    drying out, 20
    paint splashes on, 14
    pointing and jointing, 8–10
    repairing, 10
    spalling, 8, 10
    stain removal from, 13–15
    sulphate attack, 15

Carpets,
    cleaning, 26, 28–29
    grippers, 26
    stain removal, 28–29
    underlay, 25
    wear control, 26–27
Castors, 26
Ceilings,
    cracks, 31–32
    replacing, 31–33
Cellar fungus, 86
Chalking of paint, 15, 123
Chimneys,
    cold, 36
    breasts stained and cracked, 40

    leaning, 3, 37
    pointing, 3
    smoky, 35–38
    stained, 3
Condensation,
    in bathroom, 59–62, 65
    diagnosis, 73–74
    painting over, 77
Cooking stove, canopy over, 65–66
Copper, preserving brilliance of, 133
Crawling board, 1

Damp,
    from condensation, 73–76
    from faulty dpc, 73–74, 81–83
    interstitial, 73–74, 84
    from outside walls, 73–74, 78–80
    painting over, 18, 78
    from paraffin stoves, 75
    from roof, 1, 80–81
    in upstairs room, 74, 76
Doors,
    banging of, 79
    flush sheathed, 44–45
    painting, 41, 44–45
    panelled, 44–45
    removal of stains from, 14
    rising butts, 42
    sticking, 41–42
    woodworm in, 90, 93
Double glazing, 76
Downpipes,
    painting, 4, 5
    repairing, 5
    types of, 4
Draughts, 43, 76

Efflorescence, 3, 8, 20, 22, 88, 123
Electric cables, protection against wood-
    worm fluid, 98
Electric heating, in bathroom, 62
Extractor fans,
    in bathroom, 62
    in kitchen, 62, 66–67, 74

Fence posts, 135–139
Fireplaces,
    all-night burning, 39
    cracked, 38–39
    design, 37
    hearth repair, 39
Floors,
    covering,
        with carpet, 25
        with linoleum, 25, 83, 122
        with vinyl, 31, 122
    levelling, 25
    squeaky floorboards, 25
    woodworm in, 97–98
Frass, 92, 93
French polish,
    cleaning and polishing, 132
    removal, 130
Furniture,
    bleaching, 130
    chair reseating, 126–128
    cigarette burns in, 130
    colour alteration, 132
    dents in, 131
    hot plate marks on, 132
    ink stains on, 132
    kitchen and bathroom, 65
    limed oak finish, 131
    natural finish, 130
    repainting of, 128–131
    restoring polish on, 131
    wicker, 129
    woodworm in, 93

Gutters,
    cleaning, 3
    painting, 5, 6
    repairing, 5
    types of, 4

Incipient decay, 86, 137
Insulation, 75

Kitchen, decoration of, 59–60

Ladders,
    aluminium *v.* wooden, 7
    cat, 1
    extension, 6
    mounting, 6
    preserving, 7
    storing, 7

Limed oak finish, 131
Linoleum underlay, 25

Moss eradication, 13
Mould eradication, 19

Oak, removal of stains from, 14
Outhouses, painting, 13

Paints for various surfaces, 140–142
Pattern staining, 76–77
Pebbledash,
    repairing, 11
    stain removal from, 13–15
Picture frames, restoring, 132–133
Plaster,
    cracking, 22
    drying out of, 20–21
    spalling, 21
    stains on, 22
Plastering, 22–24
Plasterers' tools, 23–24
Polystyrene,
    fire retardant, 33–34
    as lagging, 98
    painting, 33
Primers for various surfaces, 142–
    143

Refrigerator repainting, 65
Rendered walls,
    cleaning, 124
    painting, 10–11
    repairing, 10
    stain removal from, 13–15
Ripper, 3
Rollers for painting, 11
Roof mending, 1–3, 80–81
Roughcast,
    painting, 10–11
    repairing, 10–11
    stain removal from, 13–15

Scaffolding (improvised),
    over bath, 60
    in room, 68
    for stairwell, 68
Sheds, painting of, 13
Slates, mending, 3
Stains,
    on inside walls, 17–22
    on outside walls, 13–16
Stairway,
    carpeting of, 70–72
    construction of, 69–70
    squeaking, 69–70
Stone, removal of stains from, 14, 15
Stucco,
    painting, 12

Stucco—*continued*
  repairing, 12
  stain removal from, 13–15
Sulphiding, 22

Tiles,
  bathroom and kitchen, 33–34, 59–60, 63
  ceiling, 59–60
  floor,
    cleaning, 31
    laying, 29–31
    removal, 31
  inside wall, 59–60, 63
  roof,
    cracked, 80–81
    painting, 3
    replacing broken, 1
Timber cladding, painting of, 12
Tingle, 3
Tyrolean finish,
  painting, 10–11

repairing, 11
stain removal from, 13–15

Wallpaper,
  advantage of, 17
  cleaning, 122
  stain removal from, 22
Walls,
  cavity, 20, 83–84
  drying out of, 20
  replastering, 22–24
  stain removal from interior, 17–22
W.C. pan, cleaning of, 64
Windows,
  cleaning, 123
  leaded, 57–58
  mending sash cords in, 48–51
  painting, 51, 53, 54–57, 77
  replacing panes, 51–55
  sills, 57, 79–80, 86
  sticking, 48
  types of, 47
  woodworm in, 93